The rewritten, up-to-date version of his best-selling book

All You Need To Know About The City

CHRISTOPHER STOAKES

KNOW THE CITY 2015/16

For Reference Only

British library cataloguing-in-publication data

A catalogue record for this book is available from the British Library.

Published by:
Christopher Stoakes Ltd
Marlowe House
Hale Road
Wendover
Bucks
HP22 6NE

ISBN: 978-0-9574946-5-7

First edition published January 2013. This second edition published January 2015.
Printed and bound in Great Britain.
Written by Christopher Stoakes. Researched and edited by Viola Joseph.
© Christopher Stoakes 2015

What this book is about

This book is a completely revised, rewritten and up-to-date version of the best-selling guide *All You Need To Know About The City*. It provides a quick and simple explanation of the financial markets of which the City of London is the leading international centre. It explains who the types of market participant are, the various financial instruments and transactions, and the different markets in which they are dealt and traded. It explains why interest rates and currencies change and touches on everything from crowd-funding to Islamic finance. It discusses the LIBOR and foreign exchange rate scandals. It covers and replaces the content previously published in *All You Need To Know About The City Part 2* and *All You Need To Know About The Global Financial Markets*.

Who this book is for

Anyone who needs to know about the financial markets for whatever reason, but specifically for students who may be thinking of working in the City and young professionals about to start their City career who don't want to appear to be asking stupid questions.

Who this book is by

Chris Stoakes is the author of a number of best-selling books on the financial markets, law, commercial awareness and business writing. Students praise them for making complex subjects easy to understand and being an enjoyable read. By profession Chris is a lawyer but he has also been a journalist, editor, marketing director, teacher on an MBA, management consultant, trainer and facilitator. He is a poet and was a scholar at Charterhouse and Worcester College, Oxford where he read law.

This book, *Know The City*, is a completely revised and rewritten version of *All You Need To Know About The City*, together with *All You Need To Know About The City Part 2* and *All You Need To Know About The Global Financial Markets*.

This book completely revises and replaces all of those. Why?

The world has moved on since Chris wrote them. The global banking crisis in 2008, the eurozone crisis from 2011 and the LIBOR and foreign exchange scandals moved the financial markets from the business pages to front page news. Many of the terms and complexities he explained then are part of the common vocabulary now.

Attitudes have changed too. The financial markets were originally a conduit through which the savings of individuals were channelled to those businesses that would put them to the best, most profitable use. But the financial markets became a place where risk was sliced, diced and sold on. It became a place where big bets were made, large amounts of money were won and lost, and individuals walked away with huge bonuses. When the music stopped the rest of us as taxpayers picked up the tab. No wonder politicians, their ears permanently attuned to what gets votes, started talking about erecting a structure of regulation that would return financial markets to their original purpose – to grow economies without rewarding recklessness.

Young people who want a career in the financial markets (for whom this book is written) want to know the true purpose of what they do. This book tells you.

It begins by looking at what happens to individuals' money when we entrust it to institutional investors. It looks at how these institutions invest our money – and in which markets – on our behalf. It looks at the intermediaries through which money is invested in the securities (shares and bonds) of issuers. It looks at who those issuers are and why they need our money.

It looks at the more complex aspects of the financial markets – complex types of debt funding, securitisation (which turns that debt into bonds) and derivatives, which are instruments and transactions derived from others. Finally it looks at the macro-economic aspects of the global financial markets, the international financial centres and emerging markets and explains the banking, eurozone, LIBOR and foreign exchange crises and scandals.

It does this in the same style and simple language that made the previous books so popular.

CONTENTS

INTRODUCTION: CODEBREAKING THE FINANCIAL MARKETS

It's your first day at work. Your clothes are starchy new. Your shoes are stiff and pinch your feet. You don't know what you're doing or where you're going. Everyone else seems to be so much more knowledgeable and confident. They must all be looking at you.

'There goes that City new bug,' they must be thinking.

Whatever you do or say, you don't want to look an idiot.

You don't want to torpedo your career – which stretches ahead of you, the weeks, the months, the years – on day one.

Relax. Read this book.

If this is you – and, don't worry, we've all been there – this book tells you what you need to know about the City, and gives you the confidence to ask questions to find out more.

Maybe this isn't you.

Maybe you're walking round the City's dark alleyways. You pause, look through an office window and see people at monitors. What are they doing?

This book tells you.

Maybe you're at Canary Wharf, craning your neck to peer up at the tall towers. What kind of businesses need that much space?

The answers are in the following pages.

Maybe you're at a dinner party and the attractive person next to you says they're 'an arbitrageur' or 'a technical analyst' or 'a trader who does cable'. What can you say that will impress the pants off them?

Read this book. It could change your love life.

Maybe you're an armchair investor, scanning the personal finance pages of the Sunday papers. You find they're written in gobbledigook.

This book cracks the code.

Maybe you're studying. You need to know about the City for your assessment. Maybe you're wondering what your studies will lead to. Maybe the City.

Read this book. Sorted.

Above all, if you're working in, or are thinking of working in, or are thinking of having anything to do with, the City, and feel overawed and stupid because you don't understand it, then this is the book for you.

Who This Book Is For

This book is aimed principally at young, fee-earning professionals in the City – **bankers, brokers, fund managers, lawyers, accountants, insurance brokers, surveyors, actuaries, PRs, recruiters** and **headhunters**, among others – who are starting out on their careers.

But it's also for **support staff** such as **secretaries, PAs and business managers** as well as people in **mid-office and back-office functions** such as **Accounts, HR, IT, business development, PR, compliance, settlement** and **custody** – in other words, professionals who are specialist in their own jobs but need to understand what the fee-earners do in order to support them in their roles. That's because for City institutions to compete these days, all of their people need to understand the business.

But this book is designed to be simple. So it's also for **students at school, college or university** who are thinking of working in the City or need to understand the financial markets for their studies.

This book isn't restricted to the young and inexperienced, either. The course on which it's based has been delivered by me to a roomful of **regulators**. Nor just to those in the City. Many people based outside London need to know what goes on in the City because it affects their work or their clients or their pensions and savings.

Health Warning

A word of warning. I've tried to make this book short, simple and easy to understand, so that you read through to the end and get the whole picture.

To do that, I've had to leave out a lot of stuff and to cut corners. Not the important stuff, though. Just the boring minutiae. Don't worry: what's in here is all I've ever needed to know in 25 years of working in and around the City.

If you know nothing, it's better to be roughly right than precisely wrong. This book helps you be roughly right.

Once you've got the basic framework from this book, you can fill it out by dipping into the *Financial Times* and *The Economist* from time to time – but only if you want to.

Right, let's get going.

Snapshot Of The Financial Markets

This book is about the City, meaning the financial markets of which London is the international financial centre. Why it is we'll explore later. For now I want you to understand the financial markets and the participants in them.

We'll start with their purpose. The **purpose of the financial markets** is to channel money to those that will use it best (this may sound odd when for a decade their purpose seemed to be to place increasingly risky bets that in the end almost destroyed the world's banking system).

Issuers, Intermediaries, Institutional Investors

The ones that want to make use of that money are **companies and governments** which we'll call **issuers**. The **banks and brokers** that help them do this are **intermediaries**. And the sources of this money are big financial institutions called **institutional investors**. The institutional investors buy **securities** issued by companies and governments (which is why the companies and governments are called issuers). The intermediaries (banks and brokers) **distribute** these securities to institutional investors and **make a market (trade)** in them so that if the institutional investors want to sell the securities at any time they can do so.

And that's it: that's the financial markets in a nutshell. Three types of participant: issuers, intermediaries and institutional investors; and various types of market in which securities are traded.

Source Of The Money

The big question is: where does this money come from that institutional investors use to buy these securities? And the answer is: people like you and me. There are three types of institutional investor: insurance companies; pension funds; and wealth managers. And they all get their money from us.

Insurance companies take in premiums and invest those premiums in the markets in order to meet claims out of the investment returns. **Pension funds** take in contributions from employees (often matched by employers) and invest that money to provide financial support for when employees retire, stop work and become pensioners. **Wealth managers** (also known as fund managers) take in money from individuals and invest it on their behalf in the markets.

Equity And Debt

The securities that institutional investors buy fall into two types: shares and bonds. Shares are also called equities and bonds are a type of debt. In fact there are only two types of money: equity and debt.

Equity is the term for **shares** issued by companies (governments can't issue shares; they have citizens not shareholders). Investors put money into a company and in return get a share in it which makes them part-owners (called shareholders). As a company makes profit it pays its shareholders **dividends** out of those profits. A profitable company is a valuable company so the value of its shares will appreciate (increase). When shareholders decide to realise (turn into money) their investment, they are hoping to sell their shares at a profit. So shareholders hope to get a dividend stream (income) and a profit (capital return) on the sale of their shareholding. The downside is that if a company goes out of business (becomes insolvent) the shareholders lose their investment: their shares become valueless.

Debt falls into two types: **loans** and **bonds**. Both work in a similar way and, together, they make up the **credit market**.

With a **loan**, the borrower is lent a **principal** amount (the amount of the loan) and pays interest on that amount until the loan is repaid. The lender gets its money back plus interest in the meantime. Loans are provided by commercial banks (what you and I would call a lending bank) which take in deposits and borrow from each other on the interbank market and lend that money out.

Bonds are like giant IOUs – 'I owe you a $100 million and will pay interest on that at 5% until I repay you the $100 million in 10 years'. Companies and governments take out loans and issue bonds. They issue bonds with the help of investment banks and brokers which distribute those bonds to institutional investors and trade them.

Loans are made in what is called the **banking market**. Bonds and shares are issued and traded in what is called the securities or **capital market** (capital means money).

And that's it. You now have the code that unlocks the financial markets. The rest of this book simply expands on what you have just read. There is a bit more to it than that, which is why this book is the length it is. But in essence, that's it.

CHAPTER 1

STOCK (EQUITY) MARKETS

Stock exchanges – public companies – listed – physical trading floors – virtual – market makers – bid – offer – bid-offer spread – turn – touch – yellow strip – Daily Official List – day order – open order – fill-or-kill – execute or eliminate – limit order – market order – stop order – jobbers – specialists – brokers – single capacity – rule book – corporate brokers – funds – collective investment schemes – units – diversifies – book building – distribution – placing – underwrite – aftermarket – sell side – buy side – private placement – primary – secondary – initial public offering (IPO), listing, floating, flotation, going public – rights issue – seasoned equity offering – pre-emption – diluted – index – FTSE 100 – average – Dow Jones – bellwether – weighted – auction – order driven – two-way prices – mandatory quote period – quote-driven – open-outcry auction – continuous auction – call auction – order book – hybrid – liquidity – trade efficiently – without moving prices against – thin market– illiquid – spread – efficient market – block trade – program trade – inter-dealer brokers – clearing – fails – intra-day – settlement – dematerialised – short selling – stock lending – fungible – false markets – junior markets – senior markets – nomads – free-floats – matched trade – stock exchange mergers – mutual organisations – incorporate – ECNs – dark pools – crossing networks – high frequency traders – aggregators – insider dealing – insider trading – market sensitive information – public domain – spike

Let's start with the capital markets. The market where shares are issued and traded is the stock market or **stock exchange** ('stock market' and 'stock exchange' mean the same). Stock exchanges are the oldest and most well-established symbols of the international financial markets. After all, a stock exchange is the quintessential trading market. It's what most non-financial people associate with the financial markets. It's certainly the case that any country keen to be seen as a financial centre sets up a stock exchange in short order.

Stock Exchanges

A stock market is simply a place where shares in companies can be bought and sold (they are called 'stock markets' because companies were originally called 'joint stock companies'). These companies tend to be large and are known as **public companies** (because their shares can be bought by anyone) or **listed** (because their shares appear on the stock exchange list). In the past a country might have more than one exchange before telecommunications made that unnecessary. Manchester had a stock exchange (the UK's main one is in London). Philadelphia in the US still has one (the principal US stock exchange is in New York). Although originally geographical in their coverage, most stock markets are now part of the international equity markets in that investors from around the world trade on them. And many, as we shall see, have merged with each other.

Some still have **physical trading floors** like the New York stock exchange where members come to trade. Others like London are purely **virtual** – members trade over the phone and onscreen and every trade has to be reported to the stock exchange. That information (which company, what volume – number of shares – and price) is then publicised by the stock exchange to all market participants via data providers such as Reuters and Bloomberg whose screens are on every market trader's desk. This means that all members receive the same information simultaneously as if they were on an actual trading floor.

Market Makers

The stock exchange will ensure that every listed share has a number of members acting as **market makers** whose job is to quote a continuous price in that share over the trading day. Having more than one ensures competition and keener prices. The price a market maker offers will reflect how many shares in that company it has. If a lot, it may be keen to sell. If too few it may be keen to buy.

Bid is the price at which a member will buy from you and **offer** is the price at which they will sell. The **bid-offer spread** is the **turn** (profit) the member makes between the two. The spread is a measure of how liquid a security is, that is, how deep the market for it is, and how frequently it is traded. The less liquid a security is, the wider the spread is likely to be. The **touch** is the best price available (buy or sell) at any particular moment. On the London Stock Exchange the **yellow strip** on screens displays the highest bid and the lowest offer prices. The **Daily Official List** is the daily record containing the prices of all that day's share trades. Typical trading and broking instructions include:

- day order = to be done today or else it lapses

- open order = remains open until done

- fill-or-kill = do it now in its entirety or else it lapses

- execute or eliminate = do as much of it now as you can and forget the rest

- limit order = do it at this price or better; don't do it if this price is never reached

- market order = at best price possible

- stop order = do it only once this price has been reached, but you can then do it at a different price (the trade can then be above or below that price).

On some exchanges there are two types of member: **jobbers** (called **specialists** on the New York stock exchange); and **brokers**. Jobbers operate on the floor of the exchange making markets in shares. Brokers come on to the floor of the exchange to carry out buy and sell instructions for their clients. Brokers are not allowed to buy or sell shares for their own account but only for clients and only jobbers and brokers, as members of the exchange, are allowed on to its trading floor. This system is known as **single capacity**. Brokers will go round all the jobbers that make a market in a specific share in order to get the highest bid price (when selling for the client) and the lowest offer (when buying).

Because brokers aren't allowed to own shares, single capacity ensures that the broker is always acting in the client's best interest and not recommending shares the broker wants to offload. In London the distinction between jobber and broker has gone and all members are market makers. In place of the safeguard of single capacity there is a detailed financial services **rule book** that sets out the basis on which a market maker acts for a client, in order to avoid conflicts of interest. Now that there is no longer a distinction the term 'broker' has come to be applied more generically to traders of shares. Many broking houses are owned by banks. **Corporate brokers** act for companies. They act as their eyes and ears in the markets, gauging investor sentiment towards them and drumming up support amongst institutional shareholders for fund raising and M&A deals.

Clients are predominantly institutional investors. In London institutional investors make up four-fifths of the investor base (private individual investors represent a fifth only and are declining). Instead individuals rely increasingly on wealth managers to put their money in pools or **funds** called **collective investment schemes**. Individuals have **units** in a fund and the fund invests in the market. The size of these funds mean they can hold a much wider number of shares than an individual could, so this **diversifies** (spreads) the risk.

Primary And Secondary Markets

Brokers and banks help companies issue shares. They do this by going round institutional investors testing the appetite for the company's shares (how many at what price institutional investors will buy) and getting informal commitments. This is called **book building**. They will then use this information to advise the company on the size and price of the issue. They will then **distribute** the new shares (**placing** shares with institutional investors) and **underwrite** the issue (agreeing to take up any shortfall so the issuer will always raise the money it expects to) and will sell any **rump** (shares left over) in what is called the **aftermarket**. So issuers and the intermediaries are called the **sell side** and the institutional investors are the **buy side**. (A **private placement** is the distribution of shares to a small group of institutional investors without using a public issue.)

The act of issuing shares is called the **primary** market. Once shares have been issued they can then be bought and sold in the **secondary** (second-hand) market. A private company's first share issue (the point at which it becomes a public company) is known as an **initial public offering (IPO), listing, floating, flotation** and **going public** – all these terms mean the same thing. It can then issue further shares through a **rights issue** (in the US a **seasoned equity offering**). It's called a rights issue because existing investors have a right of **pre-emption**: they have first refusal over any new shares in proportion to their existing shareholding so that their existing shareholding isn't **diluted** (proportionately smaller) once these additional new shares are in issue.

All stock exchanges have an **index**. It's what market commentators focus on. In London it's the FTSE 100 (the Financial Times Stock Exchange index of the hundred largest UK companies – called that because the *Financial Times* newspaper publishes it). Charles Dow, founder and publisher of *The Wall Street Journal*, took the 12 top stocks listed on the New York Stock Exchange (NYSE), added up their prices and divided by 12. The result was an **average** figure which he called the Dow Jones Industrial Average (it has since been broadened to include 30 companies). If you do that every day (and publish it in your newspaper), readers get an instant sense of how the market is moving compared to say yesterday and last week. Market commentators look at how a country's stock market is doing as an indicator of the overall well-being of its economy (known as a **bellwether**, a weird word, meaning 'indicator' or 'barometer' or 'yardstick' or 'symbol of'). The Dow Jones is now a leading indicator of how both the US and the global markets are faring. Some companies can become so big that they start to skew the index and their share price comes to dominate the index and make it less representative. So indices are **weighted** to avoid becoming driven by just a few dominant stocks.

How Trading Happens

Trading on a stock exchange is by **auction** or is **order driven** or both.

Auction is the way you and I would expect a stock market to work. Market makers are required to quote **two-way prices** (buy and sell) at which they are prepared to trade in securities throughout the trading day or **mandatory quote period** as it's called. This is called **quote-driven** trading. Where there is a trading floor it is called an **open-outcry auction** system. **Continuous auction** means they are doing this throughout the trading day.

In some markets – smaller ones where the volume of trades is thinner – a **call auction** system prevails, that is, with orders batched together at certain, specified times during the trading day to concentrate activity and ensure there is a market at all. The market maker then carries out an auction to determine the price at which trades occur. Some markets have short trading days for this reason. When the Mongolian stock market started in 1992 it only had enough volume to open for two hours one day a week. Now it manages to open every day for an hour, achieving daily turnover of roughly $200,000 on a market capitalisation of about $60 million. Trading is online. The Rwanda market, which opened in 2008 and has a market capitalisation of around $27 million, is open for three hours a day.

An **order driven** system (often called an **order book**) is based on an electronic order book in which buy and sell orders are entered anonymously. The system pairs up matching buy and sell orders for the same shares at the same price, and executes them automatically during continuous trading. Orders that aren't executed lapse or are withdrawn.

Stock exchanges can run both systems in parallel and will use an order-driven system for trading shares in larger companies where volume is high and liquidity is good (that is, there is a lot of trading in their shares). Order-driven is good for these high-volume, low-margin trades. Auction – especially open outcry – is better at accommodating complex trades in big amounts.

A **hybrid** system is one that retains an open-outcry auction (specialists on a trading floor), but alongside order-driven and electronic systems. The risk with a hybrid system is that specialists no longer have the full flow of orders and may be bypassed over time, yet they are the ones who keep prices continuous when volume is low.

Market Efficiency

Liquidity is a measure of how efficiently you can execute a trade in a market or (to use the London Stock Exchange definition) 'a measure of tradability of a company's shares'. Liquidity determines whether you can trade at all and, if so, whether you can **trade efficiently** (at a good price). The problem with stock markets is that they are sensitive to buy and sell orders: a buy order drives up the price and a sell order depresses it (the basic supply and demand of capitalism). Liquidity means how deep a market is. The deeper the market (that is, the more trades carried out) the easier it is to trade in and out **without moving prices against** you. By contrast, in a **thin market** any indication of wishing to buy or sell will start to move the market against you. If a share is **illiquid** that means there aren't many buyers or sellers so you may not find someone to trade with in the volume you want. Even if you do, the **spread** may be so wide that the act of buying or selling is itself expensive because you're selling too cheaply or buying too expensively.

When you or I go shopping, we expect to get whatever we want at the price that's marked on the packet or the shelf. Not so in the financial markets. What happens is that the price of everything is changing all the time, depending on how much is in stock and how many buyers want it. Imagine a baker's shop where the number of loaves available and what they cost is forever changing, depending on how many people are in the shop at that moment and what they are ordering. That's how the financial markets operate. In other words, your very act of slipping into the baker's to buy a loaf may move the price against you. This is why market liquidity is so important. An **efficient market** is one which doesn't move much when you trade in or out of it. So if I go into the baker's and whenever I go in they have a very limited selection and it all immediately becomes expensive, then that's an inefficient market. And after a while I may not go there anymore. So in time that market may dry up and die.

Volume Trades

Institutional investors have enormous portfolios and they don't want to buy or sell just a few hundred shares at a time. They need to trade in sufficient volume if a trade is going to have any (beneficial) impact on their portfolio's overall performance. So for big institutional investors with large buy and sell orders to execute the larger and deeper a market the better. To avoid moving the market against them they may instruct an intermediary (investment bank or broker) to do a **block trade** or a **program trade** (the latter may be done in instalments, often driven by computer to identify the optimal price at which to execute a succession of trades). These are tricky deals because they can move the markets easily. The intermediary may act as agent for the institutional investor or on a sale may actually buy the securities off the institutional investor and then gradually dispose of them in the market. The desire of market participants to keep their trades and positions secret means that there are brokers (called **inter-dealer brokers**) who act as intermediaries between intermediaries in order to keep their trading patterns discreet.

Clearing And Settlement

Once a trade is executed, it has to be cleared and settled. **Clearing** means checking that all the details of a trade match – any trade by definition involves two parties, so clearing is the action of ensuring that each party's record of the trade is the same, otherwise the trade **fails** and won't clear. Clearing takes place at the end of each trading day, but if volume is high it may happen several times a day, known as **intra-day** clearing. **Settlement** is when the trade is paid for and the shares change hands. On the London Stock Exchange this is done through a system called CREST which is a paperless share settlement system. It started in 1996 and replaced a system called Talisman (a paper-based system run by the stock exchange). It's a requirement of listing that a company's shares be eligible for electronic settlement (in other words that shares are **dematerialised**: electronic entries instead of hard-copy share certificates). When a trade is executed, details of the trade are sent by both parties electronically to CREST which matches the messages and checks there are enough shares in the seller's account to make the sale. Then on settlement CREST instructs the market maker's bank to make a payment to the seller's account. CREST then updates its own accounts to record the new shareholder's shareholding.

It may surprise you that settlement does not occur immediately after the trade takes place, but T+3 (three days after the trade) in the larger markets and as much as a week in smaller, less developed markets. This is a hangover from the days when shares were physical certificates (in the 1980s there was such a backlog on the Milan exchange that it became known as Monte Titoli, 'mountain of share certificates'). This delay in settlement allows for a crucial aspect of market trading and one that has attracted sharp criticism: short selling.

Short Selling And Stock Lending

Short selling is selling something you don't own. In normal life this would seem odd. But in the markets it's simply the opposite of buying securities. You buy because you think they will increase in price. Why not sell securities if you think they are overvalued and will go down? It's just as valid to hold a view that markets are declining (and be able to act on it) as it is that markets are going up. So short selling is selling a share you don't have in the expectation that the price will go down and the delay between the trade and settlement is what enables you to do it. Let's say you short sell a share at today's price. You can then borrow that share from someone who has it, deliver it at settlement, then go into the market and buy the share at (what you hope will be) a lower price and give that one back to the owner you borrowed it from. Providing shares to enable short selling is called **stock lending** and it earns the owner a fee from you (paid out of the profit you made from selling high and buying back low).

The people who lend shares in this way are institutional investors for whom the share in question is a long-term holding they will always want (for instance because it is a key component of the index) and for whom the fee generates additional return. Stock lending assumes that the shares involved, if not identical, are at least **fungible** (that is, their principal terms have the same economic effect). Short selling can itself, if done in sufficient volume, drive prices down. This was why in the banking crisis short selling, particularly of bank shares, was suspended. It can create a **false market**, which is the reason the authorities may prohibit it. But in actual fact it becomes self-correcting. If short selling drives markets relentlessly down then institutional investors will stop stock lending because it depresses the value of their portfolios.

Senior And Junior Markets

Many stock exchanges have **junior markets** for young or small companies that cannot meet the **senior market**'s requirements.

A stock exchange will impose certain minimum requirements before a company can list. It will do this to ensure that those companies that do list are viable (stock exchanges don't guarantee that companies listed on them are good investments; just that listed companies will be required to provide sufficient financial information for an informed decision to be taken). So, to list on a main exchange you may need a trading history of a few years, a certain level of cash flow, a certain amount of new money you want to raise by issuing fresh shares, and a commitment that a percentage of your shares will be available for public trading.

This doesn't suit companies that have little or no trading history (a biotech company may need lots of capital for research and development yet may not even have a product let alone a history of selling it); or have lumpy cash flow because of the sector they are in; or the bulk of whose shares will remain in the ownership of the founder and his or her family.

To cater for these companies – which can offer more rapid growth to investors while at the same time being riskier because they can just as easily run out of cash and go bust – exchanges set up junior markets, as they are called. These have fewer requirements so it is cheaper to list on them. Often the exchange will oversee the junior market and require one of its members to be appointed as a nominated adviser (called a **nomad**) to oversee a company that wants to list on the junior market. Companies that are successful on the junior market may graduate to the senior market (the stock exchange itself) in due course.

Junior markets have one big problem: liquidity. By definition, smaller companies will have smaller **free-floats** of shares. Fewer investors will want to buy and sell them so achieving any kind of **matched trade** can be difficult. The fewer the trades, the less consistent the price at which those trades take place. And these investments are inherently more risky so attract fewer investors anyway. So junior markets come and go with surprising frequency. Frankfurt's Neuer Markt looked poised to achieve lasting success, but closed. Similarly Singapore's Catalist exchange, launched at the end of 2007 to replace its secondary board called Sesdaq, struggled to attract new listings. The same is true of Hong Kong's Growth Enterprise Market.

London has had a succession of them: the USM (Unlisted Securities Market); AIM (Alternative Investment Market); Ofex, Plus and ISDX. China, as in many things, is not far behind. It had a pipeline of 300 companies waiting to list on its junior market, the Growth Enterprise Board, which it launched in 2009 as part of the Shenzhen exchange. Occasionally junior markets become successful in their own right. NASDAQ in the US is one of these. It originally attracted technology start-ups but has been successful in retaining them as they've grown larger.

Stock Exchange Mergers

Liquidity is an issue for all exchanges and has driven a wave of **stock exchange mergers**. Stock markets are businesses in their own right and thrive or fail depending on whether they attract enough buyers and sellers. Most start as **mutual organisations** (owned by their members) but many **incorporate** (become companies). They then go public and (a bit bizarrely) list on themselves. Over the last few years there has been tremendous competition between stock exchanges with many merging to gain increased liquidity and economies of scale (through using common clearing and settlement systems – the bigger the market, the greater the volume of trades, the lower the cost-per-trade). With electronic markets, the restrictions on trading are driven more by time zone (when the market is open) than geography (where you happen to be located when you trade). Screen-based trading makes markets virtual.

The larger and more liquid a market, the less impact individual orders have on it and the greater those orders can be. A large, liquid market is one on which buyers and sellers will converge because they know they will be able to trade at keen prices: the volume of trades means that a continuous price is available and the bid-offer spread is kept to a minimum. In other words, it is self-perpetuating: the bigger the market, the more business it will attract and the bigger still it will get. It's like any market: the bigger the market, the more buyers and sellers you have, the more trading there will be and the keener the prices will be; whereas if you just have a few people standing around they may not have anything in common that they want to buy or sell at all.

This is why it is so difficult to bootstrap a new market into existence. It's why the NYSE is able to preserve a specialist system. It is so big its physical trading floor can and, arguably, does offer a more visceral indication of market moves – you can sense it in the air and from the degree and noise of trading activity as members scream orders at each other in times of market stress – than you get just from sitting at a screen and seeing it fill with red (falling prices tend to be in red). Some argue that specialists enable large orders to be digested by the market with less disruption than through electronic trading.

The irony in these stock exchange mergers is that institutional investors which own them are also their key users. As such they are wary of vertical integration (stock exchanges owning the clearing and settlement systems) and consolidation (fewer but bigger exchanges) because the smaller the number of global exchanges the greater the risk of market dominance and monopoly providers which means they can then drive up the price of trading. In some cases clearing and settlement services have been outsourced, to avoid this degree of vertical integration which some institutional investors resist.

Dark Pools And Crossing Networks

Stock markets face competition from other sources too, such as **ECNs** (electronic communication networks) and **dark pools**.

ECNs are virtual, electronic platforms which enable banks, brokers and institutional investors – which together form consortia to start them – to by-pass markets altogether and, effectively, create their own. ECNs work by sifting through market data (posted by traders) in order to match buy and sell offers.

Dark pools, also called **crossing networks**, are unofficial markets used to trade large blocks of shares anonymously and off-exchange. By keeping these trades private they don't therefore move markets against those engaged in them (whereas a large buy or sell order on-exchange will drive prices up or down respectively during execution).

Users of dark pools say that exchanges no longer have the facility to trade large blocks of shares because electronic trading tends to break packets of shares down into small, executable orders. They also complain that stock markets suffer from **high frequency traders** (computer-driven exploiters of price variations) that move the price against them. But these networks risk splintering market liquidity which is why banks allow each other access to pools to which they belong and have got together to launch **aggregators** that search across dark pools for matching trades.

ECNs and dark pools compete with exchanges by sucking trades and liquidity away from them. Stock exchanges have been fighting back, merging with them or launching their own.

Insider Trading

Stock exchanges regulate their markets (just as much as governments do through criminal law and financial services regulation). Stock exchanges want to attract companies that want to list and investors that want to buy their shares. So they want their markets to be above board. In particular, stock exchanges are vigilant for **insider dealing** or **insider trading** – that is, buying or selling shares on the basis of **market-sensitive information** that is not in the **public domain**. Often before a corporate takeover is announced the target's share price will **spike** (go up), indicative of insider dealing. Equally, exchanges don't want their markets to be manipulated by one or more buyers or sellers who are deliberately trying to corner the market in a company's shares or are trying to control the fair price at which those shares should trade. So any exchange wants to ensure that (1) companies are transparent about what they are doing and how well they are doing; and (2) investors are operating on a level playing field and aren't trying to gain unfair advantages over each other. Although these two points are simple to make, in practice they lead to enormously complex systems of financial regulation (see later).

So far we've been looking at shares (equities) which make up the stock market. Now we're going to look at the credit market.

CHAPTER 2

THE BOND (DEBT) MARKET

Credit – credit market – credit investors – service – tax-deductible – securitisation – munis – denominations – origination – primary market – bondholders – secondary market – maturity – coupon – fixed income – FRNs – lead manager – managers – bought deal – eurobonds – eurodollars – sovereign – rescheduled – closed – treasuries – gilts – gilt-edged stock – priced off – base rate – basis point – credit rating – rating agencies – discount to face value – zero coupon bonds – nominal or par value – deep discount bonds – market value – yield – tenor – duration – redemption – risk premium – yield curve – yield curve inverting – high-yield bonds – acquisition finance – junk – downgrades – below investment grade – fallen angel – vulture funds – maturities – commercial paper – rolled over – medium term notes (MTNs) – MTN programme – long bonds – perpetuals – OTC (over-the-counter) – off-exchange – on-exchange – debentures – settlement – depositories – depository receipts – sponsored – unsponsored – ADRs – GDRs – profit-participation certificates – repo market – repurchase agreement – repo rate – covered – covered bond – reverse repo – haircut – money markets – short-term debt – certificates of deposit – bills – treasury bills – bankers' acceptances – endorse – merchant banks – Bank of England – money supply – interest rates – real value – inflation – lender of last resort – in the market – discounted – deflation

Credit is debt (loans and bonds). So the **credit market** comprises loans and bonds and **credit investors** are institutional investors that have large bond holdings.

Both companies and governments are big users of debt: companies because the interest they pay to **service** the loan is **tax-deductible** making it a cheaper form of capital than equity (by contrast, dividends have to be paid out of taxed income); governments because their only other source of income is from taxing their citizens and that isn't enough in recessions and, if excessive, risks making them unpopular. The difference between loans and bonds is that a bond is just a tradable loan. So banks make loans but the much bigger universe of institutional investors (credit investors) buy and sell bonds. The bond market is therefore much bigger than the loan market. Loans can be turned into bonds through a process called **securitisation** (it turns them into securities).

The bond markets are amongst the largest financial markets in the world. The total value of bonds in issue is about $40 trillion, of which about a quarter trade internationally and the remainder on domestic markets. The US is easily the largest single bond market with about $15 trillion in issue of which about $500 billion's worth are traded each day. Some of the biggest bond issuers in the US are states and local governments. These municipal bonds – known as **munis** – account for about $2 trillion.

How Bonds Are Issued

Most bonds are available in **denominations** of around $10,000. Few individuals buy them but any one issue will be held by a large number of institutional investors holding anything from $100,000 up to $100 million of an issue. Bond issues tend to be for several hundred million up to several billion: it's too uneconomic and unpopular (because illiquid) among investors to do an issue that is smaller.

A borrower will issue a bond with the advice and assistance of an investment bank to arrange, distribute and underwrite the issue (very similar to equities – the two processes used to be different but have now converged with banks owning brokers). This is called **origination** or **primary market** activity. Institutional investors will buy the bonds issued (so becoming **bondholders**) but then subsequently may sell them in the **secondary market** (second-hand market). As with a loan, a bond issuer will pay interest on the bond and repay the principal on the bond's **maturity**, when it expires. But because the bondholder can always sell the bond, the issuer may not necessarily know exactly who the bondholders (lenders) are at any particular moment and issuers don't keep registers of bondholders (as they are required to do of shareholders).

In the old days when bonds were physical cards and not the electronic entries they are now the interest portion would be printed as a series of coupons that had to be detached from the bond (this way you could keep the bond safely in a vault and just present the coupon to the issuer's bank to get the interest). For this reason the interest a bond pays is still called the **coupon**. Most bonds are fixed-interest bonds (the rate of interest is fixed for the duration of the bond) and so bonds are also known as **fixed-income** instruments. Those that have a floating rate of interest are called **FRNs** (floating rate notes). When a bank underwrites an issue it may create a syndicate of other banks to help it bear the risk. The first bank is the **lead manager** and the other banks are known as **managers**. Alternatively the bank may buy the whole issue itself. This is called a **bought deal** and means the issuer gets its money immediately. This convenience, and the increased risk carried by the bank (it may not be able to place all the paper having bought it all), means the cost to the issuer is higher.

Bonds traded internationally were originally known as **eurobonds**. The first international bonds in the 1960s were designed to tap **eurodollars** that had been deposited in European banks by Middle East oil exporters selling oil to the US. These were ordinary dollars trapped offshore because the US didn't want them reimported (they would have flooded the money supply system and caused inflation). So the US government levied a hefty 20% withholding tax on any that were, which kept them out of the US and meant they stayed in Europe. In time the term 'eurobond' came to mean a bond issue made outside an issuer's home country and not in its domestic currency. Now it increasingly means bond issues denominated in euros.

Sovereign Issues

Bonds issued by governments are called **sovereign** issues. Sometimes they default (Argentina in the 1980s and again recently, Russia in the 1990s) and then no one will lend to them for a while until their debt is **rescheduled**. In that period the credit markets are said to be **closed** to them.

The US government is the biggest borrower in the world yet borrows at the cheapest price (the theory is that if the US ever defaulted, that's the end of capitalism as we know it, so the US won't). Its bonds are called **treasuries** because they are issued by the US government's Treasury Department (quaintly, UK government bonds are called **gilts** or **gilt-edged stock** from when they used to have silver edges to distinguish them from the rest).

Basis Points

Many other financial instruments are **priced off** treasuries which act as a benchmark (in the way that the Bank of England **base rate** is a benchmark for borrowing in the UK). But the sums involved in the international financial markets are so big that you can't price off treasuries (or anything else) in whole percentages. You have to use basis points. A **basis point** is one hundredth of a per cent. So an issuer whose coupon is 75 basis points above treasuries is doing well since its cost of borrowing is just three-quarters of a per cent above that of the US government.

Rating Agencies

Issuers need a **credit rating** to issue a bond. This is because institutional investors that buy bonds and investment bank traders that trade them do not have time to analyse an issuer to see whether it will default on (not pay) the bond or the coupon. **Rating agencies** provide a rating and charge the issuer for doing so. The top rating is AAA (called 'triple A').

Zero Coupon Bonds

Some bonds aren't issued with a coupon. Instead they are issued at a **discount to their face value**; on maturity the holder receives the face value. So a 5-year $100 million bond issued at $80 million without a coupon (which is why they are called **zero coupon bonds**) has an implicit interest rate of 4%. This 'rolls up' the interest into the total amount that the investor gets back at the end. In some countries this interest element is not therefore subject to income tax. The face value is also called the **nominal** or **par value**. Zero coupon bonds are also known as **deep discount bonds**.

Yield

A bond's **market value** (what anyone is prepared to pay for it) will not always be the same as its nominal ('named') value (printed on it). Obviously if a $100 million bond is maturing tomorrow it will be worth $100 million today less the overnight rate for $100 million, in other words as close to $100 million as you can get. But during its life its market value will vary depending on what interest rates generally are doing and where they are heading. This is just one example of how crucial interest rates are to the financial markets.

Instead of a bond's price, traders talk about its **yield**. Yield is the interest rate a bond pays as a function of its price. So if a $100 million fixed-income bond pays 5% (that is, it pays $5 million in interest a year) and interest rates double to 10%, its market value may go down to $50 million because a bond costing $50 million that pays $5 million in interest is yielding 10% which is the same as prevailing interest rates. I say 'may' because how far down it goes depends on a number of other factors too including its **tenor** or **duration** (how long the bond has to go to **redemption** when it matures and is redeemed – paid back – by the issuer). So bond traders judge the value of a bond by what interest rates are doing and are likely to do. In this way the bond market is a predictor of where interest rates generally are going.

Generally the longer the borrowing period the higher the rate of interest (it is easier to predict that a borrower will still be able to pay tomorrow than in say ten years' time so this increased uncertainty commands a higher coupon as a **risk premium**). This means that, in general, interest rates increase with the borrowing horizon and this is called the **yield curve** (it's actually a straight line if you plot it on a chart). But in times of great short-term economic turbulence and uncertainty, when the market can't see the next six months but can the next ten years, borrowers may pay more for short-term money. This is known as the **yield curve inverting**.

Understanding yield explains the meaning of **high-yield bonds**. They are bonds that pay a high rate of interest in relation to their market price. Sometimes issuers will issue high-yield bonds deliberately. For instance, a company taking over another may need short-term finance quickly at a time when it is fully stretched. So it may raise the money through a high-yield bond in order to acquire the target, and then refinance the bond immediately after completing the takeover with a longer-term issue paying a lower rate of interest (using short-term loans and bonds in this way is called **acquisition finance**).

But there's another type of high-yield bond called **junk**. This is when a rating agency **downgrades** an issuer because the risk of default has increased. If the rating goes **below investment grade** many of the institutional investors that hold the issue will have to sell it (pension funds in particular are usually forbidden from holding securities that are 'below investment grade'). The market value of the bonds will therefore go down as fewer institutions will want, or are able, to hold them. As the market value goes down, the yield goes up hence a high-yield bond is often labelled a junk bond or a **fallen angel**.

There's money to be made in junk. Not all junk bonds default, so holding a number is less risky than holding one issue. There are **vulture funds** and traders that specialise in buying junk bonds cheap and holding them in the hope that the issuer's fortunes will recover and the bonds will be repaid in full. Or they may hold so much of a company's paper (bonds) that they end up dictating what it does (this can happen with sovereign issues too, most recently Argentina).

Types Of Bond

Bond **maturities** range from 90 days to 20 years. Bonds of very short duration are called **commercial paper**. These issues are made by large, listed companies to fund short-term financial needs. They usually have a maturity of just 90 days and don't pay interest but, like zero coupon bonds, are issued at a discount to their face value. What tends to happen at the end of the 90 days is that the commercial paper is **rolled over** – a fresh issue of debt is made to replace the paper that has expired. Commercial paper is bought by banks to park short-term deposits, but mainly by other large companies to invest short-term revenues that aren't immediately needed but will be soon.

Bonds with maturities of around five years are called **medium term notes** or **MTNs**. They are often issued as part of an **MTN programme** where the company has a panel of three or four banks that have agreed to meet all of the company's debt requirements including loans and MTNs. The company decides at any point what it needs, tells the panel and the one offering the cheapest rate gets the business.

Long bonds have maturities around ten years or more (these labels are all approximate in the markets). A small number of bonds in issue are **perpetuals** – they have no redemption date and will never be redeemed unless the issuer (usually a bank, in the case of perpetuals) chooses to retire them. Some very long bonds have mechanisms that allow interest deferral in times of financial stress, making them akin to equity.

What sort of bond to issue depends on an issuer's funding horizons, its credit standing in the market and what the market has appetite for. This will reflect where interest rates are and wider economic well-being or uncertainty. Certainly, types of bond go in and out of fashion.

OTC And Off-Exchange

Most bonds are traded **OTC** (**over-the-counter**), in other words directly between market participants (banks, brokers and institutional investors) using screens and telephones. This is a key feature of financial markets: most securities are traded **off-exchange**. Only shares and certain types of derivative (which we'll come on to) are traded **on-exchange**. It's true that a minority of bonds are listed on stock exchanges and these are traded through the stock markets on which they are listed (in the case of international bonds, these are mainly listed in Europe on the London and Luxembourg exchanges, if they are listed at all). In the UK there are corporate bonds called **debentures** that are listed on the London Stock Exchange but these tend to be domestic rather than international issues.

By and large, the **settlement** of international bond trades is different from that of shares because the bond market is international, OTC and not exchange-based. Instead, bonds are held as electronic entries by **depositories** such as Euroclear and Clearstream – each of which is owned by a consortium of user banks. In the US the major clearing house for securities trading is the Depository Trust & Clearing Corporation in New York.

Depository receipts are a form of security (share or bond) that enable it to be bought and sold in markets where it would otherwise not be available. A depository receipt occurs where a depository holds securities and then issues a separate security in respect of them. It's a way of enabling a company to access, say, the US market, without having to go through the formalities of issuing and registering securities that comply with US regulations. Instead it puts shares or bonds on deposit with a depository which then issues receipts that are themselves tradable. Where a depository receipt is set up by the issuer it is **sponsored**. Where a bank sets one up, by simply buying a company's securities in the market and putting them on deposit, it is **unsponsored**. **ADRs** (American Depository Receipts) trade in the US. **GDRs** (Global Depository Receipts) are international. **Profit-participation certificates** are similar: they are like shares but have no voting rights.

Repo And Money Markets

We've talked about the impact of interest rates on bond markets. The link between bonds and interest rates is even more explicit in two key markets that link economic policy with the financial markets: the **repo market** and money markets (of which the repo market forms a part). Repo is short for **repurchase agreement**. A repurchase agreement is a simple contract under which I sell you a bond for £X and agree to buy it back in three months' time for £Y. Essentially what you are giving me is a secured loan: the purchase price (£X) is the loan, which you will get back when I buy the bond back in three months; and the interest element is £Y (the price I will pay you in three months' time) less £X (the amount you paid me) which is called the **repo rate**. Because it is a genuine sale-and-purchase agreement, you have title to the bond. So if I fail to buy it back you simply sell it in the market, so you are completely **covered** against my credit risk. The **covered bond** market works in a similar way. In a **reverse repo** the seller is a bank that buys securities in return for providing cash.

Repos are used by institutional investors and banks to gain short-term liquidity by harnessing long-term assets (the bonds in question tend to be government securities such as US treasuries or UK gilts where the underlying risk of default is minimal). The amount that you will lend me on the bond is lower than the face value of the bond in order to cover any fall in its price over the three-month period and this difference is known in the trade as the **haircut**. The benefit to you is that you are investing cash risk-free and, if you think the securities will go down in value, you can sell them in the market and buy them back at a lower price just before you need to deliver them back to me. The repo market is very sensitive to rates and bond prices. It is also a critical source of liquidity. It is a cross between stock lending (an institutional investor activity) and money lending (a commercial banking activity).

Repos are one type of instrument found in the **money markets**, which are markets where **short-term** debt instruments are traded, such as commercial paper, interbank loans and deposits (called CDs because they are evidenced by **certificates of deposit**), treasury bills (short-term bonds are called **bills**; **treasury bills** are issued by governments) and instruments called **bankers'**

acceptances. In the old days banks would **endorse** (guarantee) merchants' bills (tradesmen's IOUs) at a discount to their face value and these became known as bankers' acceptances (and the banks that did it as **merchant banks**).

Controlling Interest Rates

The **Bank of England** will buy some types of bill including short-term UK government bonds and bankers' acceptances. It also enters into repos in respect of gilts (longer-term government bonds). By buying these instruments the Bank of England introduces money (liquidity) into the market. By selling them, it reduces (soaks up) market liquidity. Doing so has a direct impact on the amount of money in the **money supply** system which in turn affects interest rates: tightening liquidity increases interest rates because money is less readily available.

Controlling **interest rates** and the money supply are key jobs of the Bank of England. Interest rates are the risk-free return that cash will give you. If interest rates go up, people will put their money on deposit at banks. If interest rates go down they will take their money off deposit and invest it elsewhere. So the markets are always looking ahead at where interest rates are going. In general, increased interest rates discourage people and businesses from borrowing so act as a brake on economic expansion. Reduced interest rates encourage borrowing and economic growth. This suggests that low interest rates are best. But if interest rates are too low, too much borrowing leads to too much money chasing existing investment and spending opportunities. This makes prices go up so it costs more to buy the same things. This means that in effect the **real value** of money (not the nominal value printed on it) has gone down (it will buy less than before).

Inflation

This is called **inflation** and encourages even more spending (before prices go up even further). Inflation discourages savings and investment and hits those on low fixed incomes such as the poor, the unemployed and the elderly particularly hard. Government therefore tries to minimise inflation by controlling interest rates. But increasing interest rates too rapidly chokes off lending and stunts economic growth. So it is a fine line.

Interest rates are set by a country's central bank, which is part of government (the Bank of England isn't a bank as you and I understand the term). The central bank also acts as **lender of last resort**, supporting banks that go bust. Otherwise people wouldn't entrust their money to the banking system and companies and government wouldn't be able to borrow that money.

Strangely enough, when it started in 1694, the Bank of England was a private company. It was not part of the state at all. It helped the government borrow until the government's borrowing dominated the market to such an extent that the interest rate the government paid became the market rate: the market had to accept whatever the government was prepared to pay ('Owe a banker a thousand pounds and it's your problem; owe him a million and it's his'). The Bank of England was nationalised after World War Two, because its role was of such national importance. Originally any bank in England was able to print its own notes (which operated like bankers' acceptances or letters of credit). By the time it was nationalised, the Bank of England had been given this lucrative monopoly, another reason for it to be in public ownership.

What Happens When Rates Rise

When the Bank of England increases interest rates, the following things happen:

- The *stock market goes down*. Money deserts the stock market to go on deposit at banks where the rate of interest on offer is now, in relative terms, more attractive. So the stock market goes down. Companies' *cost of borrowing goes up* so their profits will go down which also makes the stock market go down.

- *Bond prices go down*. This is because they are now offering a less attractive rate of interest so they will go down and their *yield goes up to* match the increased rate.

- The *pound sterling goes up* because investors around the world who want to put their money on deposit in the UK to gain these more attractive interest rates need to convert their money into sterling and this demand pushes sterling up.

- A stronger pound means UK exports are more expensive for others to import so *exports go down* and corporate *profits of exporters also go down* (which contributes to the stock market fall).

When interest rates go down the exact reverse happens:

- The *stock market goes up*. Money deserts bank deposits where the rate of interest on offer is now, in relative terms, less attractive. Companies' *cost of borrowing goes down* so their profits will go up. So the stock market goes up to reflect both these things.

- *Bond prices go up*. This is because they are now offering a more attractive return. But their *yield therefore goes down*.

- The *pound sterling goes down* as international money leaves UK sterling deposits because rates of interest are now less attractive.

- A weaker pound makes UK exports cheaper internationally so *exports increase* and corporate *profits of exporters also go up* (which contributes to the stock market rise).

However, this doesn't always happen. If the Bank of England has been signalling to the financial markets for some time that interest rates will move up or down, the markets may not react at all. This is because they are always forward looking so the expected change may already be **in the market**, that is, **discounted** in current prices. And if markets approve of the move, they may move in sympathy. The financial markets hate it when policy makers do not appear to be in control. So if interest rates don't move up in response to inflation, they worry.

Note that a little inflation is all right. It has the effect of gradually increasing asset values (e.g. house prices) and reduces the real value of debt which increases the feel-good factor. The opposite of inflation – **deflation** – is worse: consumers don't spend because they know the price of goods and services will be cheaper tomorrow – but then they don't buy tomorrow either, because prices will be lower still the following day, so demand dries up. Industry falters, the economy grinds to a halt and the real value of debt increases. Deflation like this is difficult to get out of. Japan was in a deflationary environment for over a decade (known as Japan's Lost Decade) and interest rates fell to zero – because no one wanted to borrow.

CHAPTER 3

CURRENCY MARKETS (FOREIGN EXCHANGE OR FX)

Currency market – foreign exchange – FX – virtual OTC – self-regulating – counterparty risk – Herstatt – net amount – netting – daily volume – CLS Bank – intra-day netting – cable – spot or cash market – carry trade – intervene – reserve currency – gold – flight to quality – devalued – the FX rigging scandal

Talk of the pound sterling brings us to another huge market: the **currency market**, also known as **foreign exchange** or **FX** for short.

Virtual OTC Market

The forex market is a **virtual OTC** on-screen market where big institutions and governments buy and sell currencies (those that are freely transferable). All major companies that do business round the world need to convert receipts into their home currency. They may borrow in their home currency (where they can get the cheapest rate) then convert that into the currency of whichever local territory they are expanding into. Institutional investors need FX to invest around the world. Intermediaries need a place where they can convert currencies that they have received from issuers or investors.

Despite its size or maybe because trades are for such large amounts, the forex market is dominated by the world's largest financial institutions. They trade with each other. How big and creditworthy you are determines whether they will trade with you. So the market is said to be **self-regulating** because no single government or regulatory body is in control of it. Banks are sensitive to the risk of other banks defaulting ever since a German bank called Herstatt defaulted in 1974 owing over half a billion dollars in incomplete forex trades. Since other banks had entered into forex deals on the basis of those with Herstatt, the forex market came to a standstill and it took weeks to unravel banks' positions.

Netting

This **counterparty risk** is known in the forex market, not unreasonably, as **Herstatt risk**. Over 150,000 forex trades take place around the world every day and many of these may take place at different times of day between the same banks. Instead of handing money over each time they trade, these banks agree to wait till the end of the trading day, tot up who owes what to whom and then only the difference (the **net amount**) is actually paid over from one to another. This is called **netting** and also helps reduce Herstatt risk.

The amount traded every day (the **daily volume**) is over $1 trillion, a third of which happens in London, making it the world's largest forex market (no wonder there are several hundred banks in London). So big is the forex market that a special bank called **CLS Bank** (Continuous Linked Settlement meaning throughout-the-day netting also called **intra-day netting**) has been set up in New York expressly to settle forex trades between over 50 of the world's largest banks, so eliminating Herstatt risk almost completely.

Spot Or Cash Market

FX is the only financial market where something is always going up. In share and bond markets, everything tends to fall together in response to wider economic factors (such as interest rate moves or expectations of moves). But in the FX market currencies trade against each other so if one is going down that means the counterpart trade is going up because currencies move in relation to each other. **Cable** is the name for the dollar / sterling trade. If the dollar goes down, then a pound will buy more dollars so sterling is up. Unlike share markets, trading in FX is for immediate settlement (buying and selling currencies for delivery now) which is called the **spot** or **cash** market. The **carry trade** is the name given to a common FX strategy of borrowing in a strong currency, buying a weaker one and riding its rise, the profit from which is greater than the borrowing cost.

Governments are big users of the forex market. Each country through its central bank amasses reserves which it will hold in a combination of currencies including its own, gold and those of the leading economies. Governments may use their reserves to buy their own currency in the market if it weakens. When they do this they are said to **intervene** in the forex market.

Reserve Currency

For the last half-century, the US dollar (the 'greenback') has been the world's **reserve currency** meaning that more international trades and deals are done in the dollar than any other currency. But it hasn't always been. Two thousand years ago it was the denarius (Rome), then the solidus (Byzantium) and in the seventeenth century – when the Dutch dominated international trade and finance – the guilder, followed by sterling (Britain) till the 1950s. Today the dollar accounts for two-thirds of global foreign-exchange reserves because the US is a large and stable economy, with open, deep and liquid financial markets and low inflation. So people have confidence in the dollar as a store of financial value.

Confidence is important to the financial markets. In the past, people treated **gold** – a singularly useless mineral but with the advantage of rarity – as the ultimate store of wealth. Even nowadays in times of global crisis, the value of gold soars as people move their financial assets back into it (called a **flight to quality**). After all, the test of any currency is whether others believe it to be worth more than the paper it's printed on.

Risk Of Devaluation

The US is also the world's biggest borrower and China holds more US debt (treasuries – US government bonds) than any other country. If the US **devalued** the dollar – in other words, actively lowered its value against other currencies (which may happen anyway if people start to doubt the US's ability to repay this vast debt) – this debt would diminish in real value, as would the value of the rest of the world's dollar deposits.

This makes people nervous. If they gradually moved their financial assets into another currency the dollar would lose its status. What that currency might be is anybody's guess: maybe China's (the 'redback').

The FX Rigging Scandal

The **FX rigging scandal** involved collusion between currency traders at different banks in the run-up to what is called the 'fix' (the point at which a currency's rate is fixed for that trading day).

The fix is important for a much wider array of market users than just the big banks that dominate the FX market. For instance, fund managers need agreed currency rates at which they can value their portfolios. Multinationals need to know the currency rates when setting local prices at which they will buy raw materials and sell finished products around the world.

The fix is a reflection of the trades immediately leading up to it. It should therefore be an impartial reflection of the volume of orders to buy and sell a particular currency. But by sharing information about customers' orders (which should have remained confidential) and either netting off or transferring those orders between each other, traders at different banks were able to manipulate the transactions leading up to the fix, so rigging the fix itself.

This mattered because although currency traders (like equity brokers) provide a separate buy and sell quote, their banks provide corporate customers with a fixed mid-market rate. Whether a bank makes or loses money on this service depends on what the fix turns out to be. Hence the temptation to rig it.

Because the size of FX trades is so big – routinely running to hundreds of millions (in the case of dollars or sterling) – even a fractional increase in or lowering of the fix (running to the third or fourth decimal point) can give a bank a profit of hundreds of thousands of dollars or pounds on a single trade. Extrapolate this out to weeks and months and you can see why the fines imposed on banks were in billions of dollars.

One of the debates the FX scandal sparked was the extent to which such markets should be allowed to remain off-exchange and OTC. The risk of bringing such markets on-exchange – as with equity markets – is the lack of liquidity. Users value the ability to trade at will, which an OTC market provides. There is more on market regulation at the end of the book.

CHAPTER 4

DERIVATIVES

Derivatives – derived from – forward transaction – hedging – speculation – underlying – cash market – hedge funds – interest rate swaps – synthetic – counterparty risk – matching trades – off-setting – currency swaps – master agreements – trade compression – credit default swap – credit event – protection-seller – reference point – put option – self-referenced – gain exposure – credit-linked notes – plain vanilla – structured product – tax rate swaps – asset swaps – equity swaps – total return swaps – property swaps – swaption – option – right – not the obligation – strike – in-the-money – exercise – out-of-the-money – American – European – Bermudan – break-even – intrinsic value – traded options – exchange traded – call option – gearing – physically settled – cash settlement – covered options – naked options – covered warrant – convertible – warrant – embedded – trading strategies – forwards – futures – locals – cash settled – offsetting – clearing houses – margin – mark-to-market – Nick Leeson – Barings – margin calls – cross-margin – gearing – contracts for difference – spread betting – long of – naked risk – stock index futures – exchange traded funds – dynamic hedging – portfolio insurance – portfolio protection – arbitrage – arbitrageur – equilibrium – price discrepancy – pricing anomalies – index arbitrage – proprietary trading – covered interest arbitrage – triple witching hour

Derivatives are instruments that are **derived from** shares, bonds, currencies and other instruments or transactions. For example, a currency trade can be for delivery at a later date. This is called a **forward transaction**. You would do this if you were concerned that the currency you want is going to go up in price before you need it. So you buy it now at today's price for delivery on an agreed future date ('forward'). This is called **hedging**: you're hedging against the risk of the currency appreciating.

Derivatives can also be used for **speculation**. They can provide massive exposure to a particular market more easily and cheaply than using the **underlying** (the instruments from which they are derived, often called, confusingly, the **cash market**). If these positions go wrong the consequences can be severe: Nick Leeson destroyed Barings Bank, his employer, in 1995 through buying futures on the Singapore futures market. Because derivatives can create enormous exposures they can dwarf the underlying from which they are derived: at this point trading in the derivatives markets can drive (affect the price of) the cash market rather than the other way round. **Hedge funds** are a type of institutional investor that are called hedge funds because they use derivatives. But they use derivatives to increase risk (speculate) not to reduce it (hedge). So hedge funds don't really hedge.

Swaps, Options And Futures

There are three types of derivative: swaps, options and futures (although, just to complicate things, a swap is really just two futures put together).

Swaps

The commonest and simplest swaps are **interest rate** and **currency swaps**. The first swaps were interest rate swaps. Let's say I take out a mortgage of £100,000 at a fixed rate of 5%. You too have a mortgage of £100,000 but at a floating rate of interest which is currently also 5%. We each pay £5,000 a year in interest. Why would each have done the opposite of the other? In some markets one form of borrowing is easier or cheaper than the other; or we may each have had the choice but had different views of where interest rates were heading. Or I was on a low income and wanted to fix my cost of borrowing to give me peace of mind, whereas you were happy with a variable-rate mortgage because you wanted to be sure that you were getting the market rate of interest however high or low that might have been. No matter, that's what we each did.

Interest Rate Swaps

Now let's say each of our views or circumstances have changed. I am now earning more so am less concerned to fix the cost of my home loan. I'm now more interested in getting the variable market rate. Or I believe interest rates are heading down for the long term. In your case you think they're going up. Or you now want to fix your cost of borrowing because you have tight cash flow and want that certainty of borrowing cost. There are various ways of doing this:

- We can each pay off the existing home loan by taking out a new loan with the desired type of interest rate. But this can be expensive. Our respective lenders will charge all sorts of fees to let us do this. Or:

- We can each service the other's debt: I pay your interest payments and you pay mine. But our lenders might notice and not like it. Also each is exposed to the other's credit risk. You may fail to pay my interest one month and cause me to default. Or:

- We can each continue to service our own debt but treat each other as if we have swapped, then every so often settle up between each other as if each were holding the other's debt. This way our respective lenders don't know and we're not dependent on the other person paying our debt. This is an interest rate swap. It leaves our existing borrowings in place but achieves synthetically (artificially) the opposite. How?

Let's say interest rates go up and over the year are at 6%. Over the year I pay £5,000 (fixed rate) and you pay £6,000 (floating rate). At the end of the year you have paid £1,000 too much and I have paid £1,000 too little, so I pay you £1,000. This means you have paid net £5,000 (as if you were on a fixed rate) and I have paid £6,000 (as if on a floating rate).

An observer might say that you did a good deal and I did a bad one. But that's not so. I got what I wanted under the swap, although I paid £1,000 more than I would otherwise have done. And if we enter into the swap for a number of years then some years I'll do well and others you will, depending on interest rates.

But the point is that each of us will have got what he or she wanted: me, a floating rate of interest; you, fixed. You can begin to see that each of us has a **synthetic** position achieved through a derivative, in this case an interest rate swap.

Role Of Banks

In real life, you and I wouldn't deal directly with each other, for two reasons: first, **counterparty risk** – neither knows whether the other will be good for the money at the end of the year; second, what are the chances of our finding each other with each of us offering the mirror image of what the other wants in relation to home loans of exactly the same amount? Answer: nil. So for these two reasons each of us would in fact prefer to deal with a bank. Initially banks only entered into **matching trades** (they would only enter into a swap if they could find an **off-setting** one to enter into as well). But swaps are now so tradable, because of the degree of standardisation, and the market is now so deep, that the bank doesn't need to keep a **square book** (where the deals offset each other).

Currency Swaps

A **currency swap** enables a company to raise funds in one currency (such as its home currency where, because it is known, the cost of funding may be lower) and then swap the proceeds into another currency which it wants to use (for instance to expand into another territory such as an export market).

So with a currency swap there is (1) an agreement to an initial exchange of currencies at the current spot (cash market) rate and (2) a simultaneous agreement to reverse the swap at a later date but at the same currency rate, regardless of intervening currency rate changes. Unlike an interest rate swap, the principal amount in a currency swap does pass between the parties (because the company wants the actual use of the other currency) and then back again on termination. The benefit for the company is that any intervening movements in the currencies' respective values are neutralised. As with interest rate swaps, banks usually stand in the middle or act as counterparty in a currency swap.

At the end of the deal, the principal amount is swapped back. In the meantime the company is servicing its home currency debt but receives a payment if, without the swap, it would have been worse off. As with the previous example of the mortgage swap, although there is a winner and a loser, each is getting (synthetically) what it wants: the other's position.

Market For Swaps

Although swaps are created OTC (over-the-counter) by banks for companies and governments, they are now so standardised that there is a huge, deep and liquid secondary market in which they can be traded. The value of swaps outstanding is over $500 trillion and daily volume is over $5 trillion. The majority of swaps are interest rate swaps. Half of all swaps trading occurs in London. Swaps became standardised – and, hence, highly tradable – thanks to ISDA which started in 1985 as the International Swap Dealers Association and introduced standardised documentation to the market. This was so successful that its remit was widened and ISDA now stands for the International Swaps and Derivatives Association.

ISDA documentation allows banks to enter into **master agreements** with each other. These master agreements cover all their swaps trades with each other. This speeds up the market (prior to ISDA, it often took weeks to document a deal) and allows banks to net off their exposures to each other (remember Herstatt risk?) meaning that deals in the same currency between two banks are aggregated and the amounts owed cancelled out until there is a single amount owing from one to the other. This keeps their exposure to each other (the counterparty risk) to a minimum. Apart from netting, a more recent innovation is **trade compression**. This means analysing a bank's trading book and replacing offsetting agreements with new ones that reflect a netted position.

Credit Default Swaps

A slightly different type of swap is the **credit default swap** (CDS). CDSs enable lenders to isolate and reduce the risk of a borrower defaulting. Let's say Bank A makes a loan to Borrower B. Let's say Borrower B's credit-rating falls or Bank A is overexposed to B (it felt obliged to lend more than it wanted to, to maintain the customer relationship with Borrower B). Bank A enters into a CDS with Insurer C for which Bank A pays Insurer C a premium. Under the CDS, if Borrower B defaults, Bank A can require Insurer C to make good Bank A's loss. In other words, the CDS will pay Bank A by reference to B's default which is the **credit event** that triggers the payment from Insurer C to Bank A under the CDS. This means Bank A has got rid of its exposure to Borrower B while retaining the loan (this may be important if Bank A doesn't want to upset Borrower B by being seen to sell the loan to someone else). It's called a CDS because it's to do with a loan (credit) going wrong (default) and is a transaction where a premium is paid (swapped) for protection against Borrower B defaulting (for this reason Insurer C is called the **protection-seller**). It's a derivative because it is derived from the underlying loan from Bank A to Borrower B.

It's possible to calibrate a CDS so that it isn't just an actual default that triggers the CDS (which, short of insolvency, is the most extreme) but, say, a deterioration in B's credit standing (a downgrade in its credit rating). In other words the risks involved in making the loan can be isolated. So far the **reference point** is Borrower B. But it could be by reference to other things: a fall in an index, for example. This is how flexible a CDS can be.

Bank A has bought from Insurer C a **put option** – that is, if the loan goes bad Bank A can put it (transfer it) to Insurer C or, at least in economic terms, be treated as if C were now the loan maker (options are explained next). Insurer C may hedge its position by – oddly – buying protection from Borrower B which thus, strangely enough, earns a fee for not defaulting. This is called a **self-referenced** credit default swap.

CDSs allow insurers to **gain exposure** to the banking market without being banks – another synthetic position created by derivatives. Insurer C is prepared to write the CDS because it is gaining exposure to Borrower B. Insurer C may want this exposure to diversify its own risk. It may like the industry Borrower B is in but has no exposure to it, because it can't lend to B because it isn't a bank. Regulators of banks and insurers keep the two and their activities apart.

Other Uses Of Swaps

There are **credit-linked notes** which combine a CDS with a bond (they have a coupon, maturity and redemption). These are used by institutional investors to hedge against rating downgrades or defaults. Almost every bond issue is made with a swap involved: either an interest rate or currency swap. Straightforward bond issues without swaps are called **plain vanilla**; a bond with a derivative involved is called a **structured product**.

There are plenty of other swaps these days, such as **tax rate swaps** (exchanging one tax position for another). But swaps aren't limited to exchanging liabilities. There are also **asset swaps** where parties exchange the return on assets: for example, **equity swaps** where returns on different portfolios are exchanged; and **total return swaps** (where all the cash flow such as interest or dividends are paid to the holder as if it held the bond or share directly).

Take **property swaps**. Institutional investors are big holders of commercial property. But a drawback of real estate investment is that it is extremely illiquid. Buying and selling commercial property can take weeks or months rather than minutes or hours. Property swaps overcome this. The party that wants to reduce its property exposure (a long-term property investor such as an institutional investor) pays part of its return from a particular property or portfolio (rent or an amount tied to a property index) to a party that wants to increase its immediate exposure (a property developer that doesn't want to waste months going through long-winded property purchases) which, in return, simply pays annual interest on the notional value of the assets swapped. The developer is betting that property returns will increase at a higher rate than it could get from a bank. Each has avoided the usual property costs (legal, tax and agents' fees) while acting on their view of the market much more quickly than if trying to complete an actual property transaction.

Swaps can even be combined with other derivatives: a **swaption** (option on a swap) allows the holder to enter into an interest rate swap and is used to swap fixed-rate cash flows that are irregular where one party doesn't want to do the swap unless some market condition (risk) happens. Swaptions are themselves traded.

Options

The second of our three types of derivative is the **option**. An option is exactly what it says: it gives you the **right** to buy something but **not the obligation** – in other words, you don't have to. Let's say shares in Exoil PLC (a fictitious public petroleum company – PLC means public limited company) are trading at £3 each. They may go up or down but if they go up – because of the discovery of a new oil field – I want to make sure I don't completely miss the boat. Instead of buying shares, I buy options. Each option allows me to buy a share in Exoil at £3.30 and costs 10 pence. £3.30 is the **strike** price.

Options usually last three months. If over that time Exoil's share price goes above £3.30 the option is **in-the-money** and I will **exercise** it. If not, it is **out-of-the-money** and I'll let it lapse (if the shares are, say, at £3.25 and I want them I'll simply buy them in the open market rather than exercise the option because under that I have to pay £3.30). Some options can be exercised at any time (**American**), some only on expiry (**European**) and some only on specified dates (**Bermudan**) – these terms have nothing to do with geography; they are just market labels. Now, certain things flow from this option trade.

- I always know at any point what my worst possible loss is (10 pence per option).

- I will only make a profit once the cost of the option is factored in (that is, if I exercise the option above £3.40 which is my **break-even**).

- The option itself has an **intrinsic value** that will go up as the underlying shares do (as soon as the share price goes above £3.40, the option itself will start to rise in value) which means I can sell the option itself for a gain (depending on how long it has to go before expiry – once expired it is worthless). Many options are created principally to be traded over their lives: these are called **traded options** and tend to be **exchange traded**, for example on the stock market where the underlying equity is listed.

- The option (this one is called a **call option** because it entitles me to call for the share) locks in a *maximum* I will have to pay to buy the share – however high Exoil shares go I will have locked in any gain above £3.30. (I could do the opposite – buy a put option that entitles me to sell Exoil shares at the strike price, which means the strike price is a *minimum* below which, however badly Exoil shares do, the price I get for them will not fall.)

- I have **synthetic** exposure to Exoil – that is, I do not own the shares but I can participate in any upside as if I did.

Gearing Effect

Options have another aspect: **gearing**. Let's say that instead of buying an Exoil share at £3, I buy 30 options at 10 pence each with a strike price of £3.30 and the shares go to £3.45. If I had bought an Exoil share my gain would be 45 pence. If I exercise the options my gain will be £1.50, that is 30 options x £3.45 market price minus £3.30 strike = 15 pence, less the cost of the option (15-10) = 5 pence = 30 x 5 = £1.50. Don't worry about the maths: the point is that by using options I made a profit of almost four times what I would have done by owning the underlying share. True, if Exoil had stayed the same and I therefore didn't exercise the options and they expired unexercised, my loss would have been £3 (the cost of all 30 options). But if I had owned 30 shares in Exoil I would have had to have invested £90 (not £3). And I would have made a paper loss of £9 if they had gone down just 30 pence to £2.70. Instead I had £87 to invest elsewhere in the meantime. This is the gearing effect of options (also called **leverage**).

Cash Settled

Options like many derivatives are not always **physically settled** (I don't ask the option seller for the Exoil shares). Instead he pays me what I would have made if (1) I had exercised the option, (2) he had delivered the share and (3) I had then sold it in the market – this is called **cash settlement**.

By dealing in the options market I avoid transaction costs in the physical or underlying market such as stamp duty (tax on share trades). Besides, the derivatives market is more liquid and efficient (cheaper to deal in) than the cash market.

Option Writers

Who would sell me such an option? Answer: institutional investors (the same people who stock lend to allow short selling). If I'm a big pension fund and will always hold Exoil shares because they give me sectoral exposure to a key market (oil) then I can afford to write options because some are exercised (so I hand over shares or pay the cash settlement) and some aren't (so I don't, and keep the option premium). Provided more expire than are exercised I will be earning useful premium income from my portfolio of Exoil shares. If I write options where I hold the underlying shares the options are **covered options**. If I don't and I would have to go into the market to buy the shares to deliver them, I am writing **naked options** and am a naked option writer. A **covered warrant** is a short-term exchange-traded option (call or put) aimed at retail investors.

Embedded Options

You can see that a **convertible** (a bond which allows the holder to switch into the issuer's equity at a pre-set price) and a **warrant** (a bond that entitles the holder to buy shares in the issuer or another company) are really just bonds with an option **embedded** in them to buy equity at a certain price. So each is a bond with an embedded equity option. A convertible pays investors a lower rate than an equivalent bond, because it gives them the right to convert it into shares if the issuer's share price rises above a certain point. The benefit to the issuer is a lower rate of interest with the possibility of redeeming the bond through issuing shares – which costs it nothing.

Trading Strategies

Options lend themselves to use in combinations which create **trading strategies**. Here are some examples.

- *Straddle* = simultaneously buying or selling both a call option and a put option with the same strike price. This strategy works when a market remains within a particular trading range or band. The trader is expecting a lot of price volatility but isn't sure in which direction.

- *Strangle* = straddle with different strike prices for each option. This is where the trader thinks volatility is more likely to be in one direction than the other.

- *Strap* = a combination of two call and one put options. The trader thinks a price rise is the more likely but has the protection of the put option.

- *Bull spread* = buying and selling an option at different prices: used where the trader expects only a modest increase in the underlying so gives up part of the potential upside to recoup part of the premium.

- *Bear spread* = opposite of a bull spread: used where the trader expects a fall in the underlying but caps the downside risk.

- *Cylinder* = buying an option while selling (writing) one at a different strike price – the effect is to offset the two premiums, reducing the cost while reducing the upside.

- *All-or-nothing* option = the trader receives a fixed price if the underlying reaches the strike or goes above it.

- *Butterfly* or *alligator spread* = combination of a bull and bear spread where the premium receipts and payments cancel each other out, so (in theory) it costs nothing.

- *Condor spread* or *top hat spread* = a trading strategy that limits the downside and upside – through buying and selling calls at increasing strike prices. A variation is called the *Christmas tree spread*.

I hope you can see that options are versatile instruments that provide great flexibility and are relatively risk-free for the trader (in that the maximum loss is the premium and is always known, right from the outset). Compare this to futures.

Futures And Forwards

The final types of derivative are forwards and futures.

A **forward** (short for forward contract) is simply a contract to *take delivery* of something at a *fixed date* in the future for an *agreed price*. Because it's a contract that is delivered and paid for at some point ahead of the present, no actual cash changes hands until maturity. The critical point about a forward is that it is an obligation to make payment and take delivery whereas an option gives you the right but not the obligation.

Forwards – OTC

Forwards are traded in the OTC market. Forwards have their origins in the commodity and currency markets and can be traced back 3,000 years. Originally they were a way for producers (of foodstuffs such as wheat, sugar, cocoa, coffee, tea and so on) to sell their crops forward, so guaranteeing a return on planting, nurturing and harvesting their crop. For consumers it was a way of locking in a price in advance. The effect was to smooth out peaks and troughs in natural production (if the harvest is too good, producers suffer because the price they get goes down; if the harvest is poor, consumers have to pay a lot more because of scarcity). It means a cocoa farmer can lock in a sale at a price that will return a profit; and makers of chocolate can keep prices constant to the consumer without supermarkets having to alter prices from week to week.

This explains why the biggest futures markets in the world started in Chicago (the agricultural crossroads of the US) in the 1850s in response to a series of bad grain harvests. Although the majority of instruments traded there now are financial derivatives, they have their origins in agricultural produce, which is why commodities are markets in their own right.

Futures – Exchange-Traded

A **future** is simply a *standardised forward* that is traded *on-exchange* in a futures or derivatives market. As soon as a contract is for a specific amount of cocoa (say 500 kilos) of a certain quality (drinking chocolate quality) you have a standardised contract that can be traded on an exchange. This is a future. They tend to be three-month contracts. The terms 'futures market' and 'derivatives exchange' are synonymous now since most futures markets have expanded to embrace other types of financial derivatives such as exchange-traded options.

Futures go up and down in value depending on (1) what is happening in the underlying commodity market and (2) how long the future has to go to expiry. These contracts (like traded options) therefore take on a life and value of their own and are heavily traded. **Locals** are futures exchange members who trade for their own account. They are like market makers, buying and selling contracts all the time, which makes futures markets liquid and efficient.

Let's say I am a local and you are a drinking-chocolate manufacturer. You want to lock in a ceiling for the price of cocoa, to cap the price you'll have to pay for it so that you don't have to increase the cost of the packs of drinking chocolate that you sell to consumers. You buy cocoa contracts (each for a sack of standard weight and quality of cocoa) from me for delivery in three months' time at $100.

In three months' time the price of cocoa in the underlying or cash market is $120. In theory a future can be settled by physical delivery but in practice they are **cash settled**. So, for each contract, instead of actually giving you the cocoa (which I could buy in the underlying commodity market for $120 and deliver to you), I pay you $20 ($120–$100). You now buy cocoa in the cash market at $120 a sack. But the $20 I hand over to you compensates you for the fact that you are having to pay $20 more per sack than you had wanted: indeed, as a result of the $20 the effective cost to you is still $100 per sack, just as we had bargained. So you're happy.

But what about me? The chances are that I have entered into an **offsetting** trade. A producer, worried that he might not get buyers for his cocoa if there is a glut, sold futures contracts to me at $90 a contract. In this way he locked in a floor below which the price he would get for his crop would not drop. In the event the cash price is $120 (this is what he is able to sell his crop for in the underlying market). So he hands over $30 per contract to me ($120–$90). He has forgone that super-profit on his crop but has had the peace of mind of knowing that he would get $90 for his crop whatever the market price. If in fact the price of cocoa had fallen below $90, I would have had to pay him the difference. So for him the futures trade has provided peace of mind.

You can begin to see that futures enable producers and manufacturers to smooth out spikes in demand and supply. They also enable speculators (locals) to bet on the likely future moves in supply and demand. Locals can enter into a variety of offsetting trades to cover their positions. These trading strategies can be complex.

In the above example, the loss on my trade with you was $20 a contract (a fifth of the contract value). But it could have been worse. If the cash price had risen to $150, then it would have been $50 in relation to a contract price of just $100 – that's half. This is one of the downsides of futures: they can lead to huge losses relative to the principal. We'll return to this in a moment.

Clearing House

Of course the one risk in all of this when you are dealing with contracts that are only settled in three months' time is counterparty risk: how can you be sure the other person will still be around in three months' time and will honour his or her side of the trade, especially if it goes against them and in your favour?

Futures exchanges tackle this through **clearing houses**. As soon as two parties do a deal, it's cleared through the exchange's clearing house: the clearing house steps in as the counterparty to each side of the trade; so the counterparty for each is now the clearing house, not the other; in this way the clearing house isolates each from the other.

What the clearing house requires parties to do is to put up **margin**, that is, a deposit. To avoid any nasty surprises at the end of the contract, the clearing house requires each participant to keep that margin topped up if the price of the contract moves against them. If a position deteriorates over the three-month period the party concerned is required to **mark-to-market**, that is to make good that loss by increasing the margin.

Margin Calls: How Nick Leeson Broke Barings

This is what happened to **Nick Leeson** who famously brought down **Barings**, the UK merchant bank, in 1995. He ran out of margin and so was unable to mark-to-market. Leeson was holding futures contracts on the Nikkei 225 (the Japanese stock market index) which he was buying through Simex, the Singapore futures market. He was doing it because an options straddle (see earlier) on the Nikkei had gone wrong (a straddle works when a market remains within a particular trading range or band).

An earthquake that hit Kobe and Osaka in January 1995 depressed the Nikkei 225 to such an extent that it was trading well below the straddle's range and the bank's options position was badly out-of-the-money. By buying more futures, Leeson was hoping the Nikkei would recover and – possibly – that his activity would have a positive impact on the cash market and put the option back in-the-money.

When the Japanese market continued to fall, Leeson's futures contracts exposed him to that fall without any get-out (unlike options from which you can walk away on expiry). He had to mark-to-market but his futures positions were so big and so in debt that when Barings ran out of cash to meet the margin calls, the Simex clearing house had to step in and close out his positions (cancel them by using the margin to pay off the other side to each trade). Barings was bust. The market went on to recover. If Leeson had been able to hold on his trades would actually have come right in the end.

Regular users of futures markets maintain accounts with the clearing house. As futures fluctuate in value, **margin calls** are made. If my futures positions gain in value, margin is credited to my account and I can withdraw it. If my positions fall in value I have to top it up. Major participants (such as banks) are allowed to **cross-margin** between accounts held on different futures exchanges.

Gearing Effect Of Futures

The ability to trade on margin is what gives futures their dramatic **gearing** or leverage effect (similar to the gearing effect of options). Margin is what you put up by way of deposit when you enter into a futures trade. Buying a futures contract is a bit like buying a house with a mortgage: you put up a deposit and borrow the rest.

Say you have £100,000. Let's say you buy a house for £100,000 and over a year it increases in value by 10%. You sell it and you've made £10,000. Supposing instead you use £10,000 of that as a 10% deposit and borrow the other £90,000. Ignoring the interest you have to pay on the loan (this example is merely to show the impact of gearing) your deposit would have produced a gain of the same amount (£10,000).

Better still, let's say you use all £100,000 as a 10% deposit, borrow £900,000 and buy ten houses. After a year you'd have a gain not of £10,000 but of £100,000.

But since you don't actually want a house (you're going to sell after a year) you could enter into a contract that is the economic equivalent of house ownership and which says: *This contract is worth £1 million of residential real estate and expires in a year.* If by then real estate has increased in value the seller will pay you the gain. If real estate has declined in value, you pay the seller the loss. This means it is cash settled rather than settled by delivery of the underlying (houses).

This is in fact a forward or, if bought on an exchange, a future. And it can be valued by reference to a residential real estate index (say, an index of central London prime residential real estate). Now you're a futures trader.

This gearing effect echoes that of options. It means that by using a derivative you can achieve a much bigger position in the market than if you bought the underlying: by buying the derivative on margin, you in effect just need to put up a deposit rather than the full price.

It's this amplification effect that makes derivatives so powerful (and potentially dangerous – when you get into a futures contract like Leeson you don't know how far it may fall). Volumes in derivatives are now so great that they dwarf the underlying or cash market; in other words, the market value of derivatives is greater than that of the underlying to which they relate – to the extent that on occasion the derivatives market drives the price of the underlying, rather than the other way round. This is one reason why financial markets can be so volatile and why the highs and lows have been so extreme. It's also why Warren Buffett, one of the most famous investors in the world, described derivatives as 'financial weapons of mass destruction'.

Market Exposure

Gearing is one benefit of futures. The other is exposure to a market without – in the terminology of derivatives – owning the underlying. The contract on the fictitious index of central London prime residential real estate gives you the same exposure as if owning the underlying (the property itself) but without actually doing so. This has two benefits.

First, transaction costs: you'd have to buy the property with all of the associated lawyers' and surveyors' fees plus stamp duty; and to sell it you'd need an agent and lawyers again; and in the meantime you'd have to repair it and pay local rates. A single bit of paper is much easier.

Second, liquidity. Once you've bought the property it's a fairly illiquid asset – you can't sell it there and then and get your money out immediately. But a contract, especially if it's a standardised exchange-traded contract and valued by reference to an accepted index, can be sold readily.

This is why taking a position in the derivatives markets can be preferable to holding the underlying. It is this versatility combined with liquidity and low transaction costs that have given derivative markets such volume – and worry people like Warren Buffett who believe that real markets should be driven by economic fundamentals and not by the instruments derived from them.

Spread Betting

Futures are also known as **contracts for difference** and in their retail guise – where they are sold to individual investors rather than institutional buyers – that is often what they are called. The investor and broker agree to exchange the difference between the price of an asset at the beginning and at the end of the contract. The property example (above) is not quite as fanciful as it may seem. There are brokers offering property-related hedges or 'hedgelets' as one broker calls them.

These are based on another retail-oriented derivative trade: **spread betting**. The broker quotes a range or spread for the future price of an index (such as a stock or property index). The investor bets on whether it will end up higher or lower than the spread suggests. For each point that the index moves in the investor's favour, his profit is multiplied by his stake. For each point it moves against, the loss is multiplied by the stake. Say a broker quotes a spread of 5000 to 5100 on the Emerald Index (a fictitious index) and the investor bets $10 for every point above 5100. If the Emerald Index moves to 5200, the investor's return is $10 x 100 = $1,000. The investor can also bet the market will fall (shorting it) by betting $10 for every point below 5000.

Returning to property, if you own a house, betting that the market may fall may offset some of the gain you'd make if property prices rose, but will protect you if the market does fall. In this sense, any property owner (whether he or she knows it or not) is betting on property prices going up by being **long of** property: this is called **naked risk** (unconscious risk). Far better, these brokers argue, that you take that risk consciously and hedge against it.

Stock Index Futures

Nowadays you find futures in all sorts of markets: bond futures, currency futures, commodity futures. In oil, for example, oil companies use them to protect against falls in the price of oil and airlines to protect against an increase. However, the most exciting futures are on financial instruments and transactions, such as **stock index futures** (SIFs). SIFs provide institutional investors with great flexibility in the management of their equity portfolios.

A SIF is a single contract that represents an underlying index. If I want to invest in the FTSE 100, I can buy each and every one of the hundred shares. Or I can buy a single FTSE 100 futures contract by paying margin. Now, on the face of it, the future will give me each of the underlying shares at the end of three months. In practice I simply receive money if the underlying index (the cash market) has gone up or I pay over the difference if the FTSE 100 has over that time gone down. I can then roll over my position: take out a new stock index future for another three months. If I keep on doing this, I have a position in the FTSE 100 without actually owning any of the underlying.

Moving in and out of stock markets is cumbersome, the mechanics of which can wipe out the projected return. Commissions or spreads in the futures market are significantly lower than in the underlying market and the futures market is more liquid so there is less risk of moving prices against you when you trade. An institutional investor's nightmare is wanting to gain exposure to a market (knowing it is likely to move up) but finding the physical act of investing is too slow and inefficient to execute the strategy quickly (meaning that he or she is out of the market just when they want exposure to it). SIFs allow investors to gain market exposure more rapidly – through a single trade rather than individual trades in scores of stocks in the underlying cash market on an exchange.

SIFs also enable an investor that holds a substantial share portfolio to keep it while exploiting short-term market declines by selling the future: there's no need to exit the cash market just because you think it may go down, if you need to be invested in that market over the long term (such as a UK pension fund investing in major UK equities which it will hold for years). Instead, using SIFs enables institutional investors to **reduce** their exposure to a stock market without having to sell the shares in their portfolio (they keep the portfolio but sell the SIF) or gain rapid exposure to a stock market (before it goes up) without the time-consuming job of having to buy the underlying shares (which might mean they miss the rally).

Exchange Traded Funds

ETFs (exchange traded funds) are, like SIFs, based on stock indices. They are funds in which investors buy units with each unit representing a stock index or basket of shares. ETFs are exchange-listed so carry a continuous quote (unlike unit trusts and mutual funds which are priced once a day). ETFs are not derivatives but some are synthetic: they don't invest in the underlying but their returns come from a swap with a bank. The bank pays when the underlying position goes up and is paid by the ETF when it goes down.

Dynamic Hedging

SIFs allow **dynamic hedging**. A pension fund that wants to divest itself of a share portfolio (for instance to meet pension liabilities) but fears the market is falling can sell the SIF to fix the value of the portfolio at the current market price, buying itself time to unwind its cash positions at an orderly rate. This – and the act of using SIFs to fine-tune investment performance – is called dynamic hedging.

One example of dynamic hedging is **portfolio insurance**. By using SIFs, an institutional investor can continually adjust the stock/cash mix of its portfolio in line with movements in the market to give the portfolio maximum exposure to equities (which, historically, give the best return) without taking on the attendant risk. As the equity market rises, assets are switched out of cash (the risk-free or reserve asset class, usually money market instruments) into equities (the risky or active asset) and as the market falls the reverse is done. If the market keeps falling there comes a point when the portfolio is entirely in cash – which is why this technique is called portfolio 'insurance' (which has nothing to do with real insurance) or **portfolio protection**. This point can be set in advance as a floor below which the portfolio will not fall (even if the market does) because the portfolio no longer has any equity exposure. The disadvantage is that the switch back into equities lags the market so misses out on the immediate gain as the market rises. This is because the portfolio is progressively switched into equities in response to the market's upswing and not in advance of it. But the great attraction is that it does not require any market judgement or forecasting. Just to be complicated, the result is like being invested in shares while having a put option whose strike price is the same as the pre-set floor.

The use of currency futures can also help isolate the risk an institutional investor is running. For example, the institutional investor may have an expert stock selector in the Japanese market. So the actual individual Japanese shares in the portfolio are good and the institutional investor wants to hold them long-term. But if the US market as a whole looks more attractive, the institutional investor can sell the Nikkei 225 future (so keeping the Japanese stock selection without the Japanese market's risk) then go into the US market by selling the yen currency future for dollars to get the US cash to buy the S&P 500 future (the largest, most liquid future on the US stock market). This way the institutional investor retains the best stock selections (Japan) but also gets the best market and currency return (US).

Arbitrage

Derivatives can be used for **arbitrage**. An **arbitrageur** is a market professional who exploits a pricing anomaly between different markets or instruments and, by buying the cheaper and selling the more expensive, brings both prices back into line.

At the beginning of the book I mentioned buying bread in a bakery. Imagine for a moment that I discover that the same loaf of bread costs £1 in London, but £2 in Manchester. If I were an arbitrageur I would buy lots and lots of loaves in London at £1 and take them to Manchester where I would sell them for £2. Now, initially, I would make a lot of money but three things would happen. First, a lot of other people would start copying me (it's easy money). Next, the demand for loaves in London would be so great that the price would move up. Finally, there would be such a supply of loaves in Manchester – more than was immediately needed – that the price of loaves would come down. So **equilibrium** would be established between the bread markets in London and Manchester with loaves trading at the same price (say £1.50) in each place.

This is what arbitrageurs do. They scan markets looking for any **price discrepancy** and then buy and sell between two markets until there is no gain to be made because the price discrepancy has been 'arbitraged away'.

This is especially true of the futures markets, which allow market professionals to exploit **pricing anomalies** between the future and the underlying. If one is higher or lower than the other, an arbitrageur can exploit the difference by selling the high one and simultaneously buying the low one. The act of doing so brings the two back into line (equilibrium) while allowing the arbitrageur to pocket the difference. **Index arbitrage** (betting on anomalies between index prices and futures contracts) is regarded as one of the least risky forms of **proprietary trading** (when banks and brokers trade on their own account and not for clients).

Covered interest arbitrage is a trading strategy that exploits the way interest rates affect exchange rates by deciding whether, say, to put money on deposit in sterling at UK interest rates or dollars at US interest rates.

Triple Witching Hour

Like bonds, whose market value converges with their face value as they reach redemption, futures converge with the underlying as they reach expiry. But such is their volume that they can drive the price of the underlying. This means there can be twitchy times in the markets when futures, options and options-on-futures are surging towards a common expiry date as their prices and those of the cash market converge, with arbitrageurs working all three (underlying, futures and options). This can send markets into spikes and freefalls – so much so at times that the point at which these things converge has been dubbed in Chicago the **triple witching hour**. It can be like landing a plane in a storm – a bumpy ride with massive market gyrations before the plane finally touches down in one piece (you hope).

We've now covered the main international financial markets – shares, bonds, currencies and derivatives. Now we're going to look at securitisation which turns loans (not always tradable) into bonds (highly tradable).

CHAPTER 5

SECURITISATION

Regulatory capital – BIS – loan book – synthetic securitisation – sale and transfer mechanisms – financial engineering – structured finance – SPV – conduits – line of credit – tranched – sub-prime – foreclose – originate-to-distribute – toxic tranches – negative equity – interbank funding – bail out – nationalise – public ownership – income stream – whole business securitisation – receivables – retail finance – multiple-tranche structures – subordinated – reverse inquiry – collateralised debt obligations (CDOs) – credit arbitrage – Russian dolls – static – dynamic – actively managed – substitution – structured investment vehicles (SIVs) – asset backed securities (ABS) – mortgage backed securities (MBOs) – off balance sheet (OBS) – dual recourse – cash flow CDO – market value CDO – synthetic CDO – collateralised loan obligations (CLOs) – commercial mortgage-backed securities (CMBS) – negative convexity

Securitisation makes the capital of the (bigger) bond market available to the (smaller) banking market. It does this by taking bank loans that may be inherently untradable and turning them into bonds (securities, hence securitisation).

Loans are at the heart of the banking market. They are made by commercial banks (institutional investors aren't banks so aren't allowed to lend). This market is much smaller as a source of funding than the bond markets. But by turning loans into bonds, securitisation enables institutional investors to buy what were originally bank loans. This provides banks with fresh money so they can continue lending. In this way the bond markets are tapped to provide additional funding to the banking market.

Securitisation was invented about 25 years ago by a bunch of clever investment bankers at Salomon Brothers (now part of Citigroup), at the time one of the top financial institutions in the world. Their mission was to package up bank loans and sell them to institutional investors.

Regulatory Capital

This is because commercial (lending) banks face an issue. They have to maintain a cushion of capital. They aren't allowed to lend out all the deposits they receive or the money they borrow from each other. They have to hold some back. This is so they have some cash in hand to meet any withdrawals by depositors. If depositors ever feel they can't get their money back they won't deposit it.

But this is dead money. It's not money a bank can use. In fact it's worse than dead, because it has a cost to it (interest paid to depositors or other banks). So a bank lends as much as it can and is then unable to lend any more unless it tops up this **regulatory capital** as it's called. It's required by national regulators (usually a country's central bank) as well as international regulators (committees of central bankers).

You might think banks wouldn't mind this: once you've lent all you can, you sit back and collect the interest as it comes in. But banks generate other income around lending: arrangement fees, prepayment fees, drawdown fees (**drawdown** is when a company actually wants the money) and these sources of income dry up unless a bank continues to lend.

Loan Books

So the question the bright brains at Salomons (and I'm sure other investment banks – Salomons just happened to be first with the solution) had to grapple with was: how can a bank continue to lend without having to set aside even more regulatory capital? One way of framing this issue is: how can a bank sell off its **loan book**? If a bank can do this, then it can use the proceeds to lend all over again without having to add to its regulatory capital, because that cushion is now free to support a new book of loans. The only problem is: the only people capable of understanding, valuing and therefore wanting to buy a loan book are other commercial banks; and they have loan books of their own to get rid of; so they won't want yours too. The other problem was that (at least back then) loans were not easily transferred without telling the borrower, which could damage the bank-borrower relationship.

This was when the light bulb came on: if institutional investors could be persuaded to buy bank loans, the huge liquidity of the bond market could be tapped to feed the banking market (the banking market is the loan market). Before I explain how Salomons did this, I need to add two riders: (1) what they achieved you can now do with nothing more complicated than a swap (swaps were only just being invented when they did this) to create a **synthetic securitisation**; and (2) loans are themselves tradable these days (nowadays market-standard loan documentation incorporates **sale and transfer mechanisms** as a matter of course). So this explanation is a long way round the houses which you don't need to do any more. But it is a fascinating insight into real **financial engineering** (or **structured finance** which uses the **tranching** mechanism of securitisation that I'm just on the point of telling you about).

Securitisation Structure

Essentially what Salomons did was to create the following mechanism:

- Set up a **special purpose vehicle** (SPV). SPVs are companies established for a single purpose (also known as **conduits**). They tend to be in offshore markets like the Cayman Islands where the tax rate is low or nil, because additional tax on a securitisation's cash flow would make it non-economic.
- The SPV buys the bank's loan book.
- At the same time the SPV issues bonds to institutional investors.
- The money paid for the bonds by the institutional investors is used by the SPV to pay the bank for the loans.
- The bank no longer owns the loans (this is critical otherwise securitisation doesn't work).
- The SPV appoints the bank its collection agent so that borrowers continue paying interest and repayments to the bank but the bank simply passes them on to the SPV.
- The borrowers are none the wiser.

In addition Salomons had to invest huge time and effort in satisfying institutional investors, bank regulators, accountants and tax inspectors that this actually worked. The Salomons bankers did two things to make the structure palatable to institutional investors.

Enhancements

First they picked loans that in those days were regarded as the best you could have: home loans. The idea was that the last thing good borrowers default on is the loan for their house (this was before the sub-prime fiasco when loans made to poor – sub-prime – borrowers were securitised, went bad and they walked away). These particular home loans had the additional benefit of being guaranteed by the US government. So they were the best you could get. But if there were any defaults the bank (which had chosen the borrowers in the first place) paid for an overdraft at another bank to make good any loss (through something called a **line of credit**). This meant institutional investors would not face any losses if borrowers defaulted.

Second the Salomons bankers **tranched** (sliced) these home loans. They divided them up according to likely maturity. Few people who take out a mortgage stay in the same house until the mortgage is paid off. They move around, sell one home and buy another. The Salomons bankers allowed for this by dividing the loan book up into different maturities (they used computer analysis of prior home loan books to determine this statistically). They then offered institutional investors bonds of several maturities. As home loans were redeemed the repayments were rolled up to meet the redemptions of the next maturity of bonds.

These securitisations were an enormous success. Institutional investors regarded them as almost risk-free. They bought the bonds from the SPV which used the money to buy the loan book whose interest and repayment streams serviced the bonds and repaid them. The bank was then left with a whole pile of new money and an empty loan book so it could start lending all over again. And then when that book was full it could securitise it and do it all over again, and again, and again.

In fact so successful was the concept that institutional investors became comfortable with securitisations of riskier loans such as car loans, credit card debts and the like where there was no underlying security (a mortgage over a home). So much so that these days most loans are securitised.

The Sub-Prime Crisis Of 2008

Unfortunately this was taken too far and led to the banking crisis of 2008. It was caused by home loans being given to borrowers that should not have been offered them in the first place. They were called **sub-prime** (prime meaning good and sub-prime meaning less-than-good). At the time interest rates were low and US real estate prices were rising rapidly. So if borrowers did default, a lender could **foreclose** (get the property back) and sell it at a profit into a rising market. But this exuberance led to a practice called **originate-to-distribute**: you make loans knowing you are going to securitise them so you won't be around to pick up the pieces; this means you don't care who you lend to. These securitisations were distributed widely which meant that bonds backed by US sub-prime home loans started turning up all over the world.

The banks doing the securitisation tranched the loans according to how creditworthy the loans were. In fact the best tranches of sub-prime borrowing were better than average since these tended to have few defaults (the collective pool is actually safer than any individual mortgage because if you make a single loan to a borrower and he defaults, you've lost the lot; but if you've bought a bond that is backed by a thousand mortgages and a few of those default, then the percentage impact is minimal). But the worst tranches were so bad that the banks couldn't get rid of them. These **toxic tranches** as they became known came back to haunt them.

The party wouldn't have stopped but for gradually increasing interest rates (you will know why now: to stop inflation and damp down the housing market). The increased mortgage costs caused borrowers to default, the real estate market to be flooded with foreclosures and the values to start to fall.

This prompted more defaults as struggling borrowers realised they now owed more than the house was worth (this is called **negative equity** – equity is a similar concept to being a shareholder in a business; here the value of the house less the loan is your equity). So they walked away. This meant more property was on the market, which depressed values further and so on.

In the end US real estate went into freefall and banks holding toxic tranches were left with bonds that were worthless. So many banks around the world were holding so many of these now worthless bonds that banks became suspicious of each other's credit standing. So they stopped lending money to each other and one after another banks went bust (through lack of **interbank funding** to support their loans, which meant they ran out of cash).

Governments had to step in and **bail out** the banks. Otherwise, if depositors had lost money they would have taken their deposits out of good banks too and the whole financial system would have collapsed. In many cases governments had to **nationalise** the banks – take them into **public ownership** by becoming their owners.

This meant taxpayers ending up owning these bust banks and being responsible for their debts. The cost had to be met by all of us citizens through increased taxes and cuts in public services. Meanwhile businesses suffered because banks had no money to lend to help businesses expand.

Other Examples Of Securitisation

However, the basic concept of securitisation is still good and in fact you can securitise any **income stream** into a lump sum. You can securitise the income stream from a business (it has to be a steady income stream) and use the resulting lump sum to buy the business itself. The target's future income streams are securitised to provide the capital to buy it. This is called **whole business securitisation** and is an example of acquisition finance.

Rock stars, who want the present-day benefit of future royalties that stretch decades into the future long after they are likely to be dead can turn these future royalties into a present day capital sum through securitisation. Football clubs have been able to afford expensive players by securitising the revenue the club will earn from televised games and future gate receipts, and using the lump sum to make exorbitant signings (and many have found to their cost that by over-mortgaging the future for the present they go bust).

Other examples of **receivables** that have been securitised include hire payments under hire purchase agreements.

Tapping the capital markets via securitisations has made a lot of **retail finance** (credit extended to individuals) available more cheaply: credit card debt, student loans, small business loans, car loans and so on. Without it, people might not find the financing they want on terms they can afford. In fact, credit card debt almost stopped in its tracks as defaults rose, securitisations stopped and cheap money was turned off.

These types of finance are no longer primarily bank-funded but are funded in the capital markets. So just at a time when banks recoiled from continuing to lend to perfectly sound businesses and individuals, preferring to shore up their balance sheets instead, securitisation became even more necessary.

Even in the housing market sensible securitisation is possible. In Denmark, when a bank lends on mortgage it is required by law to sell a matching bond. But the bank remains responsible for servicing that bond so it has a vested interest in the borrower not defaulting. And borrowers for their part can buy bonds in the market and use them to redeem their mortgage. This becomes a self-correcting mechanism. If bonds go down in price, borrowers will buy them (cheaply) to redeem their (more expensive) mortgage. The more people do this, the more the price will go back up. In this way home loans and the bonds issued to fund them remain in step with each other, in equilibrium.

Tranching

Securitisation introduced two ideas that have had a massive impact on the international financial markets. The first is tranching: the idea that you can take an existing income stream (called a **receivable**) and slice it up further. This means you can take any sort of financial instrument and divide it up into smaller tradable instruments each of which carries a different level of risk and return.

Securitisations that do this are said to have **multiple-tranche structures**, some of which can be **subordinated** tranches (which means they are inferior in credit quality and rank behind more senior tranches). This means that investors can specify exactly what credit, yield, maturity and currency characteristics they want (this is called a **reverse inquiry**) rather than wait for an issue to come along. It's an idea you see replicated in credit-default swaps that have enabled lending banks to separate out the risk of a borrower defaulting on the loan and parcel off that risk while retaining the loan. Structured finance is a way of combining instruments to create exotic risks and exposures.

On the plus side, stripping out the most senior tranche creates new securities that can be ranked more highly by credit agencies than the generality of sub-prime mortgages. This is because the top slice of sub-prime loans are much less likely to default than the toxic layer. In this way gold (a triple A rating) could be minted from tin (sub-prime mortgages) – maybe the ultimate in financial alchemy?

For Reference

Collateralised Debt Obligations

Securitisation also introduced the idea of pooling existing securities and launching a new security off the back of them. The same idea led to securities called **collateralised debt obligations** (CDOs). The term **collateralised** means supported by an underlying security – in this case the original bonds that have been put into the pool. It's possible for the pool of securities (if they are particularly good ones) to have a better credit rating than the individual originators (this is called **credit arbitrage**).

There's no reason why you can't have a securitisation of a securitisation. These are called **Russian dolls**. Securitisation pools can be **static** (the instruments and receivables in them remain the same from start to finish) or **dynamic** where securities are put into the pool and others taken out during the life of the securitisation. These latter are said to be **actively managed**. The risk is that the manager may replace good securities with less good ones (known as **substitution**).

Structured investment vehicles (SIVs) were funds put together by investment banks to buy **asset backed securities** (ABS). They were, effectively, actively managed CDOs since investors bought participations or units in them, much as an investor would buy part of an ABS or **mortgage backed security** (MBS) or CDO issue (an MBS is a type of ABS). An SIV would maintain a portfolio of these types of securities and would buy and sell them.

Although SIVs were separate entities and **OBS (off balance sheet)** from the banks that launched them, as the markets collapsed banks found they couldn't just walk away from them; or if they did their reputation with investors would never recover. So they had to stand behind them. This is what destroyed Bear Stearns, the investment bank.

Although most securitisations give recourse only to the pool of assets securitised there are **dual recourse** securitisations where the bond holder has recourse in the event of a default both to the underlying loan pool and the issuing bank. Here ensuring the structure is OBS is not the principal driver.

There are different types of credit exposure available through the CDO structure. A **cash** or **cash flow CDO** is the most basic type where the return to the investor depends on the performance of the interest and principal flows from the portfolio of underlying assets.

A **market value CDO** is where the return depends on the market value of the pool of assets. A **synthetic CDO** is where the exposure to the underlying assets is created through the use of derivatives – usually credit default swaps – rather than an actual pool.

CLOs (**collateralised loan obligations**) are issues that bundle together cash flows from loans made to highly indebted (leveraged) companies that are tranched according to risk. CMBS are **commercial mortgage-backed securities** that bundle together loans secured on commercial properties.

A complexity of some types of asset-backed bond is the way they behave in relation to interest rates. As we have seen, bond prices usually rise when interest rates fall. But with some securitisations they fall. This is because when interest rates fall, there is a risk that borrowers will repay the underlying securities in order to refinance at a cheaper rate. This characteristic (of securitisation prices falling with interest rates) has its very own market term: **negative convexity**.

Securitisations came about to increase the capacity of the banking (loan) market – which is what we look at next.

CHAPTER 6

THE BANKING MARKET

Commercial banks – retail – wholesale – syndicates – sovereign borrowers – multinational companies – casino banks – ringfencing – bank notes – goldsmiths – receipts – bank lending – bankrupt – bi-lateral – syndicated – credit risk – interbank – London Interbank Offered Rate (LIBOR) – matched funding – broken funding – cost-plus basis – margin – turn – yield protection – profit – security – secured lending – charge – guarantees – parent company guarantee – comfort letter – covenants – financial covenants – negative pledge – priority – pari passu – restriction on disposals – asset strip – financial ratios – minimum net worth – minimum working capital – interest cover – debt-to-equity ratio – accelerate – monitor – event of default – anticipatory breach – cov-lite – payment default – material adverse change – cross default – pre-packs – administrator – insolvency rules – debtor-in-possession financings – overdraft – revolver – term loan – letter of credit facility – drawdown – repayment – amortisation – balloon – bullet – on-demand repayment – fees – arrangement – drawdown – early repayment – syndicated loans – arranger – mandate – book runner – agent – sharing clause – bought deals – market flex – term sheet – trustee – leaderless credit groups – jumbo – acquisition finance – M&A – event-driven lending – leveraged – committed – hung bridges – asset finance – finance leasing – equipment leasing – lessee – useful economic life – rental – tax allowances – primary term – secondary term – rebate of rental – double dip – operating leases – project finance – non-recourse – limited recourse – project company – project sponsors – offtake – take-or-pay – turn-key basis – escrow account – OBS financing – public private partnerships (PPP) – private finance initiative (PFI) – step-in rights – completion bond – monoline insurer – political risk – export credit agencies – soft loans – co-financings – multilateral lending agencies – supranational banks – trade finance – bills of exchange – merchant banks – discount houses – money markets – bill of lading – letter of credit – à forfait market – factoring – invoice discounting

The banking (lending) market is easy to overlook when discussing international financial markets. It's the business of making loans, which is what **commercial banks** do (either **retail** to individuals or **wholesale** to businesses). Lending is the most basic financial activity in the world but also the least international. The act of taking in deposits is retail and local, a far cry from the **wholesale** markets we've seen so far. Only when the amounts being lent become huge do banks club together in international **syndicates** to provide the loan. These are done most obviously for **sovereign borrowers** (governments) and big **multinational companies**.

Bank lending is also a small part of the financial markets. Securitisation was originally designed to turn loans (inherently untradable) into bonds. It was a way of tapping the enormous capacity of the capital (securities) markets for the benefit of the smaller banking market. The banking market was also, until the banking crisis of 2008, considered the least glamorous, especially compared to investment banking – which is about launching big bond and equity issues for big issuers and then trading those securities.

Casino Banks And Retail Banks

But that's set to change. The increasing introduction of rules to split **casino banks** (the term politicians like to use to describe investment banks) and **retail banks** (which is what commercial banks do for individuals) will reinforce the value of commercial banking as a strong and steady business. The reason for the split (or the **ringfencing**) of commercial banking is because governments guarantee our deposits with commercial banks (to encourage us to put our money with them). Governments don't want to have to bail out big banks again just because their investment banking side has dragged down their commercial banking side too.

How Bank Notes And Bank Lending Started

Lending is probably the oldest form of financial transaction (so old it's in the Bible and Shakespeare). **Bank notes** began when people left their gold with **goldsmiths** for safekeeping in return for receipts. They then used the **receipts** to pay for goods and services, instead of going back to get the gold. These receipts then changed hands while the gold itself was left with the goldsmiths. **Bank lending** began when goldsmiths realised they could start lending this gold out. This was the start of commercial banking. In fact the term **bankrupt** dates from the middle ages when the bankers of Lombardy in northern Italy used to sit on benches which would be broken up if they went bust (banca rotta). They exported their banking expertise to the City of London, hence Lombard Street by the Bank of England – which just goes to show that the financial markets were international long before the modern era.

Wholesale Commercial Banking

Wholesale commercial banking (meaning lending to companies and governments) takes two forms: **bi-lateral** loans (bi = two parties: lender and borrower) and **syndicated** lending (syndicate = several banks lending to one borrower on identical terms contained in one loan agreement). Syndicated lending tends to occur where a single borrower wants more money than one bank is prepared to advance (because of the **credit risk**).

The Interbank Market

Banks also lend to each other. The **interbank** market (loans between banks) is at the heart of international banking. Banks will borrow in the interbank market to fund the loans they make to companies and governments (London is the centre of the interbank market and banks charge each other an interest rate called **LIBOR** – the London Interbank Offered Rate). The LIBOR scandal emanated from the way in which the daily rate for LIBOR is computed – by asking a number of banks for their cost of funding. Some allegedly tried to manipulate the outcome to benefit their market positions.

The interbank market is **short-term** – most commonly three-month money. So a typical bank **borrows short** and **lends long** and funds itself for each three months of the loan period by a matching interbank deposit. This is called **matched funding**. If the bank is repaid too early, it is sitting on funds on which it is paying interest in the interbank market. If it is repaid too late, it isn't able to repay its own loan. Both scenarios are examples of **broken funding**, the cost of which is put back to the borrower.

Banks lend on what is called a **cost-plus basis** meaning that they take their own cost of funds and add a profit element (their **margin** or **turn** on the deal). A lot of the clauses in the documentation are about protecting this return which is called **yield protection**, ensuring the bank covers its costs and gets its expected **profit**.

Secured Lending

Commercial banks will always seek **security** – that is, assets they seize if the borrower defaults. This is called **secured lending**. Security can take the form of a **charge** (like a mortgage) over the borrower's assets. If the borrower is a subsidiary of a group, there may be a parent company in the group that **guarantees** the loan (hence **parent company guarantee**). A lesser form of guarantee is a **comfort letter** (the parent gives the bank comfort that the borrower will not be allowed to go bust). Note that this use of the term 'security' is not to be confused with 'securities' meaning bonds and shares. By contrast, bond issues are almost invariably **unsecured**.

Covenants

In every loan agreement, the borrower makes certain promises (called **covenants**). Some of the key ones affect the way the borrower can run its business and are called **financial covenants**. They include:

- **Negative pledge** which prevents a borrower from pledging (i.e. charging) its assets to any other creditor in preference to the lending bank, and so ensures the bank retains its **priority** over later lenders.

- **Pari passu** which is crucial in a syndicated loan since it ensures that all lenders are treated the same, and the borrower can't favour one lender over another by repaying or prepaying one before another.

- **Restrictions on disposals** so the borrower cannot **asset strip**, change its business or favour some creditors over others (by handing them assets).

Events Of Default

These are accompanied by covenants defining **financial ratios** which monitor a company's financial health, such as **minimum net worth**, **minimum working capital**, **interest cover** and **debt-to-equity ratio**. Together, they set the parameters within which the borrower may operate its business. They enable the bank to **monitor** the borrower's position and **accelerate** the loan (require early repayment) if there is any breach by the borrower (called an **event of default**). However, an **actual default** is too late for the bank. It needs to be able to get in first ahead of any other lender so it has more chance of getting its money back and getting out whole. The bank will therefore insist on rights to accelerate *in expectation* of a default (**anticipatory breach**).

Prior to the credit crunch, when credit was cheap and banks were falling over themselves to lend, they would attract borrowers by offering cov-lite (**covenant-lite**) loans where some of these financial covenants were relaxed or omitted altogether.

Other key events of default include **payment default** (non-payment of interest or principal when due), **material adverse change** (fundamental change in the borrower's financial position) and **cross default** (a default under any other loan agreement is a default under this one on the basis that any default anywhere indicates the borrower is close to insolvency).

Consequences Of Default

Two features of the credit crunch when borrowers went bust were:

- **Pre-packs** – when a borrower goes bust, an **administrator** (usually an accountant) is appointed by the creditors to *gather in* the assets, *realise* them (turn them into money) and *distribute* that money according to the local **insolvency rules**, usually to the most senior creditor first and ending with the shareholders (who usually get nothing). Those with security (a charge over the borrower's assets) are able to exercise that charge and recover what they are owed from selling the underlying asset. If possible, an administrator wants to sell off the business as a *going concern* because that will raise more money for the creditors. A pre-pack is where all of this has been planned in advance (a *pre-packaged* insolvency and administration) which is how some businesses are sold off almost on the day they are declared insolvent (bust). Like *administration*, *receivership* is a form of insolvency.

- **Debtor-in-possession financings** – where insolvent companies file under US insolvency law and are allowed to carry on trading under court protection from their creditors (known as Chapter 11 after the relevant part of the US bankruptcy code). Debtor-in-possession financings occur where Chapter 11 allows new lenders preference over old lenders. This is because companies in Chapter 11 need new money in order to recover and won't get it unless the new lenders get priority over the old.

Common Banking Terms

Other common banking terms include:

- **Overdraft** – just like a personal overdraft.

- **Revolving credit facility** (called a **revolver**) – a more sophisticated form of overdraft, it revolves in the sense that the company can reborrow whatever it has repaid, by reutilising repaid amounts, called a **rollover**.

- **Term loan** – a loan of a fixed amount for a fixed period.

- **Letter of credit facility** – used in less sophisticated markets where the bank issues a letter of credit (a bit like a cheque drawn on the bank) that the company can borrow against.

- **Drawdown** – the procedure for, and moment of, actually borrowing money under the loan.

- **Repayment** of principal, usually by way of: **amortisation** – principal repaid by equal instalments; or **balloon** – if the amount of the repayment increases with each repayment; or **bullet** – all in one go on maturity (that is, at the end of the loan).

- **On-demand repayment** – the bank can demand immediate repayment of the loan suddenly and for no reason: this is what happened in the credit crunch as banks tried to shore up their balance sheets, as a result of which perfectly good businesses were driven to the wall.

I mentioned in the previous chapter that banks don't just earn interest. Lending generates all sorts of **fees**. These include:

- **Arrangement** fees – for agreeing to lend.

- **Drawdown** fees – for actually making the money available.

- **Early repayment** fees – if the borrower wants to repay all or any of the loan early.

Syndicated Loans

Everything mentioned above applies equally to **syndicated loans**. When a borrower wants to borrow more than its bank is prepared to lend, the bank will pull together a syndicate (pool) of other banks to join in the lending. Syndicated lending is the backbone of international commercial banking. It is usually a bit more expensive than a bond issue (cheaper to arrange but carrying a higher interest rate) because it is difficult for a bank to get out of a loan or sell it on once the loan has been made. So the syndicate members can be stuck with the borrower for the term of the loan and want to be rewarded for that risk (whereas a bondholder can just sell the bond in the market to get rid of that particular exposure). But there are times – depending on the yield curve, the state of the banking industry and so on – when syndicated loans are cheaper for borrowers than bonds. In any event they offer a different source of funds.

The syndicate banks will lend to the borrower on the same terms as each other using the same loan agreement but there are additional roles made necessary by the fact that the lender is not one but several banks. The **arranger** is the bank awarded the **mandate** from the borrower (the instruction from the borrower to put together the loan). The arranger commits to the borrower to make the loan, then sells down its commitment with the help of a **book runner / syndicate coordinator** (in large syndications these will be different banks) whose job is to make the syndication happen: the arranger tells the book runner how much exposure to the borrower it (the arranger) wishes to retain and the book runner gets rid of the rest. Then there's the **agent** bank which collects interest and repayments from the borrower and distributes them to the syndicate, monitors the borrower's financial covenants and administers waivers and amendments to the loan documentation.

A key clause in a syndicated loan agreement is the **sharing clause** which says that if any bank receives a payment from the borrower, it will share that payment with the other syndicate members. This is to prevent the borrower from preferring one lender over another, for instance if the borrower has a separate bi-lateral loan with one of the syndicate banks.

Loan And Bond Structures Compared

Originally, syndicated loans were arranged by commercial banks and bond issues by investment banks. They used different mechanisms. Now global banks do both, the way they are done has converged. In both cases you can have **bought deals** where the lead bank agrees to provide all the funding then syndicates to other lenders subsequently – this can be done on an **absolute basis**, **best efforts** or **reasonable basis** (the first means the bank has to; the last that it only has to use reasonable endeavours to do so and if it can't the loan is cancelled).

An example of how the syndicated loan and bond markets have converged, using similar techniques to achieve syndication, is **market flex**. The loan market has taken market flex from the bond market – it means that the final price and structure are only arrived at after market soundings have been taken (rather than being fixed prior to syndication). This is often built into the **term sheet** (the memo the lender and borrower sign which highlights the terms to be put in the full loan agreement). This means the bank can change the pricing and other key terms if necessary to achieve successful syndication.

Bond documentation tends to be simpler, more standardised and the covenants less demanding. This is because bondholders can always sell in the market if the borrower's credit-standing deteriorates, whereas traditionally lenders were stuck with a loan come what may so required more comprehensive protection. But loans can be more flexible because it is easier for a borrower to negotiate with its lenders if it gets into difficulties than for an issuer to do so with bondholders (since the issuer won't know who they are because no register is kept).

Some bond structures overcome this by providing for a **trustee** to represent bondholders' interests should renegotiation after issue be required. But appointing a trustee adds a further cost that most issuers prefer to do without. Of course, loans that are securitised into bonds suffer from the same problem (not knowing who the holders are). This means that confusion arises on the point of default because of so-called **leaderless credit groups**.

Sovereign Defaults

By definition, the most international loans are **jumbo** (big) loans for large amounts requiring syndicates of 50-plus banks where the borrower is a prestigious **sovereign** (government) borrower. All banks want to get in on that. Every so often a generation of commercial bankers has the same bright idea: let's lend to countries because they will always be there unlike corporate borrowers which can go bust, get wound up and disappear.

This rush of blood to the head happened most spectacularly in the 1980s. In 1982 Mexico defaulted (suspended payments) on its loans. This was followed by more than 70 other sovereign defaults (roughly half in Africa and half in Latin America). The sovereign debt rescheduling crisis took a decade to work through. Then over the next 15 years (1990 to 2005) there were a further 40-odd defaults, mainly African syndicated loans and Latin American bond issues (although the most spectacular was Russia which defaulted on its bonds in 1998). Sovereign defaults are nothing new: it was defaults on Latin American government railroad bonds in the 1890s that caused Barings to go bust the first time round, almost exactly a hundred years before Leeson put it out of business for good.

More Examples Of Loan-Based Funding

Acquisition finance means loans made to borrowers so they can take over other companies in **M&A** deals (M&A means **mergers and acquisitions**). As such it is called **event-driven lending** rather than general corporate lending. These takeovers can be highly **leveraged** (meaning a lot of debt supported by little equity). Whole business securitisation (mentioned earlier) is a form of acquisition finance: it's a way of turning a business's revenue stream into a capital amount which can then be used to buy that business.

Most syndicated loans are done on a best efforts basis (see above), which the arranger makes clear in its offer letter to the borrower. But in acquisition finance, the borrower will want **committed** funds. It's no good to the borrower for the bank to go into the market and come back empty-handed. The borrower has an acquisition to finance. So the bank advising on the acquisition will commit to lend the full amount if necessary but can syndicate the debt to other banks either before or after signing. In short the arranger generally makes an **underwritten** offer.

A lot of acquisition finance loans ended up as CDOs or CLOs (collateralised debt or loan obligations) – issues backed by leveraged loans. But as cheap credit dried up in the credit crunch, loans meant to provide temporary acquisition finance couldn't be refinanced so banks were left holding the temporary loans – known as **hung bridges**.

Asset finance (also known as **finance leasing** or **equipment leasing**) is a banking industry in its own right. It's a way of funding the acquisition of an asset by getting the bank to buy the asset and **lease** it to the company (called the **lessee**) that would otherwise have borrowed the money to buy it. The lease will be for the asset's **useful economic life** (say 15 years in the case of an aircraft, 20 in the case of a ship) over the course of which the lessee makes quarterly **rental payments** until the bank has recovered the cost of the asset and the implicit interest charge over the lease's length (a bit like a repayment mortgage to buy a house).

Asset finance is used to fund big bits of kit like aircraft, ships and oil rigs. It is attractive because it can be cheaper than the company simply borrowing the money and buying the asset itself. This is because the bank actually owns the asset (rather than the company owning the asset and the bank having a security charge over it). So the deal is a **lower credit risk** to the bank which it reflects in a lower **implicit interest rate**.

The bank also gets **tax allowances** for buying the asset (developed economies provide tax advantages to encourage companies to invest in plant and machinery and so remain competitive). The bank (as lessor) passes on part of the benefit of these tax allowances to the lessee by way of reduced rental payments (usually lessees don't have sufficient profits to make use of these allowances themselves whereas banks do). So the overall cost to the lessee can be a lot lower than if it owned the asset itself and bought it with a loan.

The lease contains promises (**covenants**) by the lessee to pay the rental, maintain and repair the asset, insure it, not to try to sell or charge it and not to jeopardise the availability of the tax breaks – otherwise the lease is collapsed into a loan at a higher rate of interest to reflect the loss of the tax allowances.

At the end of the **primary term** (the period that equates to the asset's useful economic life) the bank will have recovered the asset's cost and interest on it from the rental payments. So the bank has been paid out and really has no further financial interest in the asset.

If the asset has any value left it's because of the care the lessee has taken to maintain it. So the lessee can either keep using it (the lease is extended for a **secondary term** at a nominal rent) or the asset is sold and the bank lets the lessee have the bulk of any proceeds of sale by way of **rebate of rental** (the lessee can't just keep the proceeds otherwise that would imply it was the owner all along and put the tax allowances at risk).

Finance leasing is a huge industry that spans the globe. In some countries the lessor gets the tax allowances, in others the lessee. Clever lawyers and bankers can structure deals so that the bank and its subsidiary are treated as the lessor in one country and the lessee in another, so that two sets of tax allowances become available. This is called a **double dip** and is a battleground between tax authorities and bankers. As soon as one double dip opportunity is closed by tax authorities, the bankers and their lawyers discover another.

Finance leases should not be confused with **operating leases**. If you rent a car when you go on holiday, that is an operating lease: it's not for the car's useful economic life and you certainly don't expect to maintain it or insure it. The hire company does that. Once you've returned it, the hire company leases it to another holiday-maker, and so on. However, car hire companies are often themselves lessees under a finance lease which they use to fund their vehicle fleet.

Project Finance

Another type of loan-based funding and a further banking industry in its own right is **project finance**. Project financings can be immensely complex deals that take years to come to fruition. They bring together lenders from developed economies to help construct infrastructure projects in emerging economies. What makes them different from standard commercial lending is that they are often **limited recourse** or **non-recourse** meaning that the lenders will not look to (have recourse to) the borrower for repayment.

At first sight this sounds crazy – banks not expecting repayment from the borrower? But in fact it means simply that they look to the income from the project to repay the loan, not the borrowing vehicle set up to initiate the project. That's a **non-recourse** deal. In a **limited recourse** one the banks reserve the right to seek repayment from the borrower if the project income isn't sufficient.

The borrower will be a special purpose vehicle **project company** which builds, owns and runs the project once built. The **project sponsors** are the multinational companies keen to get the project off the ground, often the contractors that build the project or supply heavy plant (such as turbines) to it. Then there are the **banks** funding the project and the **government** in whose country the project is being built, which will either buy the project's output or guarantee the purchase of it.

The key to the financing is how the borrowing will be repaid. This is done through an **offtake contract** where the government agrees to buy the project's output (such as electricity) to distribute to its citizens. Not all projects have an offtake agreement – for instance a motorway operating on a toll basis simply earns money from the users, while an oil project will usually have its product sold in the open market. But where the only customer will be the state or a state agency, the offtake arrangement will be critical since it will be the sole source of the project's income and, therefore, viability – which is why the agreement is also called a **take-or-pay** (meaning that the project output has to be paid for whether or not it is wanted or used).

Most projects are built on a **turn-key basis** – after the builder has finished, the project is ready to go (like starting a car). There will be a **long-stop date** by which the project should be completed and a **drop-dead date** by when the project must come on-stream to meet the debt service and repayment projections.

Once the project comes on-stream the money earned by the project from the offtake or take-or-pay agreement will be paid first to the banks (so they start to recoup the interest and principal of their loans) and then to the project company so it can continue running and maintaining the project. So the income generated from the project is often paid into offshore escrow accounts (**escrow** means a **trust** account) over which the banks have a charge, to ensure they are paid out first.

A typical project might be a dam that creates hydro-electric power in an emerging market, a typical natural resource project; or infrastructure improvements (ports, airports, roads, bridges and tunnels); or new industrial plant projects (such as paper mills and aluminium smelters). In fact the techniques to do this, which were exported from developed economies in the 1970s and 1980s to emerging markets, have since been re-imported by those developed economies in order to build public sector projects such as hospitals, schools and roads but with private sector financing. This keeps them off government balance sheets (like securitisation, another example of **OBS financing**) so reducing the apparent level of government borrowing. They are called public private partnerships (**PPP**) and private finance initiative (**PFI**) deals.

Many of the countries in which project financings have traditionally taken place are poor credits. They may have borrowed extensively in the international financial markets and even rescheduled. So project financing is a way of continuing to lend to such countries but without lending directly to the indebted government. In this sense project financings are often ringfenced: the money must be used for the project and the project only.

A major source of complexity in a project financing is the time it takes to come on-stream. Funds will go into the project during its construction phase and will only be recouped during its operation. This means there is always a risk – compounded by the complexity of vast construction projects in markets not used to them – that the project will run out of money before it is completed. So, during the project's construction, the banks have **step-in rights** to take over the project to ensure it is finished. Having lent money once they won't want to do it again so the funds necessary to take the project forward to completion will be provided under a **completion bond** (a form of insurance) provided by a **monoline** insurer (an insurance company specialising in one line of business, namely insuring construction projects). Completion bonds are also used in the movie business to ensure a film can be finished and distributed (movies can also be funded through finance leasing – see above).

There is one other risk: that the government likes the look of the project so much it **nationalises** it. This is called **political risk** and is neutralised by a different form of insurance – political risk insurance. This is provided by **export credit agencies** (ECAs). Every developed country has an ECA which helps to finance the sale of its exports to other markets. They include US Exim (the US Export-Import Bank), the Japan Bank for International Co-operation (the Japanese equivalent) and COFACE (France). The UK one was originally called the Export Credits Guarantee Department and was part of government but has since been part-privatised.

ECAs will help companies from their country participate in major projects (often the project sponsors seeking export markets) by providing **soft loans** to the project, that is, loans on preferential terms (called **co-financings** where funding comes from commercial banks as well as ECAs) and by providing political risk insurance. **Multilateral lending agencies** (such as the World Bank, Asian Development Bank and EBRD – the European Bank for Reconstruction and Development) which are like ECAs but have a supranational remit (and are often called **supranational banks**) will become involved in major projects. Their involvement (by providing finance or guarantees) often encourages commercial banks to participate.

Trade Finance

Public and private ECAs also get involved in another international banking activity – one of the oldest (after lending) of all – **trade finance**. Trade finance is a way for manufacturers to export their goods knowing they will be paid by the importer who may be on the other side of the world and someone they've never met but only corresponded with.

Trade finance developed out of bills of exchange. A **bill of exchange** is a promise-to-pay under which a company (the buyer or **drawer**) agrees to pay the seller (**drawee**) a given sum of money at some point in the future – usually three months ahead. It's a sort of post-dated cheque. To make it more acceptable, bills of exchange were **endorsed** (guaranteed) by prominent merchants (which is how **merchant banks** started in London).

Bills of exchange are similar to bankers' acceptances (which as we have seen are also promises-to-pay issued by companies to banks in return for short-term loans). The banks resell these bills in the market at a discount but guarantee payment. **Discount houses** developed by buying bills of exchange at a discount to face value, holding them to maturity and gaining their full value. They funded their holdings of bills by short-term borrowing from banks, one of the precursors of the **money markets**. These bills were either held to maturity or sold in the discount market and brokers developed to match buyers and sellers in return for a commission.

This was how international trade grew – at a time before email or even the telephone when exporters (sellers) and importers (buyers) on different sides of the world might not know each other and business was conducted by letter. The exporter wouldn't ship the goods without being sure of payment. The importer wouldn't pay for the goods in advance without sight of them or, at least, assurance as to their quality and proof of shipping and insurance.

This is where **trade finance** houses and merchant banks stepped in. The exporter would have the goods inspected by an independent third-party agency and deposit the **bill of lading** (shipping confirmation) and certificates of inspection and insurance with its bank.

The importer would deposit the purchase price with its bank which would issue a **letter of credit** (like a bill of exchange) payable in three months' time. With the respective banks holding the money and the documentary confirmations of quality, shipping and insurance, the exchange of goods for the letter of credit could be completed.

This letter of credit could be sold in the market for immediate value at a discount (to allow for the three months before it could be presented for payment). This international market for letters of credit is called the **à forfait market** and is a form of **factoring** (banks buying debt owed to companies at a discount and recovering the full amount on maturity – allowing the companies to get the bulk of the cash owed to them earlier than they would, so helping their cash flow). A lot of businesses benefit from using factoring (it's a specialist area of banking in its own right) and a similar activity called **invoice discounting**.

Factoring and invoice discounting are used by businesses of all sizes, from sole traders and family firms up, so we are now approaching the point at which the banking market shades into retail finance – which we look at next.

CHAPTER 7

RETAIL FINANCE

Debit and credit cards – checking accounts – unsecured overdrafts – loans – mortgages – insurance – private banking – high net worth individuals – Switzerland – conflicts of interest – Islamic banking – Sharia – riba – maisir – gharar – sukuk – murabaha – ijara – ijara wa-iktina – istisna-ijara – istisna – sharing of risk – risk management tools – microfinance – microcredit – microloans – collateral – microfinance institutions (MFIs) – outreach – unbanked – sustainability – microborrowers – pre-bankable – peer-to-peer platforms – P2P loans – direct or marketplace lenders – crowd-funding – legacy systems

Retail finance is the provision to individuals (as opposed to businesses) of financial products from **debit and credit cards** and **checking accounts** to **unsecured overdrafts, loans, mortgages** and **insurance**. As such it is almost by definition a local activity: people go to banks within their own country. Occasionally a cross-border product – a mortgage denominated in another country's currency to enable people to buy holiday homes there – appears. But for the most part this sector of banking, though perhaps the biggest globally, is the most local and least international.

Private Banking

The most international part of retail finance is in fact **private banking**, a service provided to the rich (called **high net worth individuals** or high-net-worths for short). Private banking is at one level ordinary retail finance but for the very rich. But because the rich have money, high-net-worths are really deposit-makers: in return for entrusting their wealth to a private bank (and often private banks are private in that they are privately owned or are the wholly-owned subsidiaries of publicly-quoted banking groups) high-net-worths expect a level of personalised service that extends beyond gold-plated checking accounts, debit and credit cards – retail finance with knobs on. They expect to be made to feel welcome and important. But apart from that, the bulk of what they need by way of financial services is actually wealth management of the type that institutional investors do (as much as one third of the money invested in hedge funds comes from high-net-worths).

Gold-plated retail finance, wealth management and tax minimisation, all carried out under a cloak of discretion in an environment that smacks of centuries of quiet and understated tradition: no wonder the heart of private banking is and remains **Switzerland**. Swiss banks are the leaders in the field. What was once seen as a good banking fit – investment banking for its spectacular booms and busts and private banking for its steady fee-income – led big banks to move into the high-net-worth field.

The thinking was that investment banking produced financial products (bond issues, derivatives, securitisations) that high-net-worths could invest in. The first creates financial products and the second provides the buyers. But this raises huge potential **conflicts of interest** – the investment banking side wins a mandate from an issuer and then stuffs its securities into the portfolios of the high-net-worth clients of the private banking arm. As a result of these perceived conflicts, many major banks sold off their private banking business to well-established Swiss private banks.

Islamic Banking

For the future, Asia – as in many areas of the global economy and the international financial markets – is the place with the greatest potential for private banking, especially **Islamic banking** for Muslim high-net-worths. There are over 350 million Muslims in the rapidly expanding and entrepreneurial economies of India, Indonesia and Malaysia. The small proportion that are or will become high-net-worths represent a large number of individuals, many of whom are keen to buy Sharia-compliant financial products. Malaysian banks, in particular, have been at the forefront of developing Sharia-compliant financial products for high-net-worths.

Sharia is the system of laws derived from the Koran which, when applied to banking, bans the payment of interest (**riba**) and gambling (**maisir**). This is at the heart of Islamic banking. Since a fifth of the world's population is Muslim and less than one in a hundred securities is Sharia-compliant, the scope for growth is huge. Islamic banks have been around for over 30 years (Dubai Islamic Bank which began in 1975 is thought to have been the first), they are present in over 75 countries and the annual rate of growth has topped 10% for a number of years.

All Sharia transactions have to be approved by a board of scholars. There are many such boards around the world but they do not all adopt the same approach. This is because Sharia law is, like any system of law based on religious principles, a matter of doctrinal interpretation. Malaysia, for instance, which is a leading centre of Islamic banking, is regarded as liberal (which may explain in part its market position) – possibly too liberal according to scholars in, say, Saudi Arabia.

This lack of uniformity had hindered the development of global products as Muslims in different regions cannot always use products blessed under a different interpretation of Sharia. But this is changing – partly because the most prominent scholars belong to several boards spanning the globe, and partly because of the work of various Islamic financial services boards and research academies around the world. As a result, more and more Islamic instruments are globally accessible.

The ban on riba – the raising of an interest charge that doesn't vary despite fluctuations in the value of the underlying asset – complements a ban on speculation (**gharar** literally 'deception'). This rules out highly-leveraged debt, derivatives for speculation, insurance and gambling. It follows that Islamic banks don't get involved in the money markets and wouldn't have touched sub-prime although, interestingly, asset-backed securitisations (because they are based on real, tangible assets – an important principle in Islamic banking) are acceptable as are a form of asset-backed bond called **sukuk**. In fact Sharia-based principles may appeal to ethical investors who aren't Muslim since investments in alcohol, munitions, tobacco and casinos, amongst others, are not permitted.

Islamic finance is more akin to asset finance. Islamic banks don't make loans but fund assets for customers by buying the asset then (simultaneously or at a later date) selling the asset to the customer for payment at a later date with a mark-up, which is the bank's return. This mark-up or service charge is called **murabaha**. There is in fact a finance leasing equivalent called **ijara** where the asset is funded by selling a rental participation to the investor who effectively buys a share in the underlying asset, with the rental return pegged to a benchmark. Hire purchase is **ijara wa-iktina**. Project financing is achieved through **istisna-ijara** financing (**istisna** is a form of deferred vendor financing where the seller provides the loan).

The underlying concept is one of the **sharing of risk** with the attendant sharing of profit. It follows that there isn't the equivalent of the general purpose loan where a company borrows the money without specifying what it will use it for. Instead this is special-purpose funding where the amount in question is applied to a specific purpose. Sukuk securities act as securitisations, backed by an underlying asset in respect of which a return or cash flow is generated. The sukuk holder has a share in the underlying asset, receives an income from the asset and shares the responsibility for its maintenance.

There are Sharia-compliant derivatives and hedge funds on the basis that more liberal interpretations of Sharia support **risk management tools** for genuine hedging (reducing risk) and where there is a clear link to an underlying asset. This has given rise to a fledgling OTC Islamic derivatives market with the most common transactions being swaps and index-linked derivatives. Equity investment is permitted – indeed it falls clearly within Sharia principles of risk-and-reward sharing but with restrictions on the types of business that can be funded. Because of the demand for Sharia-compliant equity investments, a number of Islamic market indices have been launched as benchmarks on western markets such as the New York and London stock exchanges.

London is the market leader in Europe for Islamic finance and claims to offer a substantial cluster of expertise in the City, with over 25 banks, 10 fund managers and several international law firms with specialist Islamic banking practices. The UK is the only western country that features in the top 10 list of countries with the largest amount of Sharia-compliant assets ($10 billion). By contrast, New York is a small and insignificant player with, so far, little appetite from its investors for Sharia products. Dubai is the hub of the Islamic banking world, followed by Bahrain. Beyond the Gulf, Malaysia and Singapore are the largest centres for Sharia finance. Malaysia dominates the sukuk (bond) market, accounting for an estimated two-thirds of the worldwide market.

Microfinance

Another type of retail finance sweeping parts of the world is the antithesis of private banking. **Microfinance** is the business of providing financial services to vast numbers of poor people in developing economies. **Microcredit** is the provision of tiny loans (**microloans**) to poor individuals to spur entrepreneurship. These individuals lack **collateral** (assets on which they can borrow), steady employment or a verifiable credit history. They cannot meet even the most minimal qualifications to gain access to traditional financial services.

Microfinance has been a success story since starting in the 1970s, pioneered by Grameen Bank in Bangladesh. Microfinance was seen as the private sector successor to state-owned agricultural development banks. They had been present in developing countries from the 1950s, providing subsidised agricultural credit to small and marginal farmers in hopes of raising productivity and incomes. But in this they largely failed. During the 1980s, microenterprise credit concentrated on providing loans to poor women (considered a safer and more conscientious customer base than men) to invest in tiny businesses, enabling them to accumulate assets and raise household income and welfare.

There are over 4,000 **microfinance institutions** (**MFIs**) serving over 150 million people in 100 developing countries, with about $30 billion out on loan and $15 billion in deposits. Seven out of 10 are in Asia and two out of 10 in Latin America. The bulk of MFIs are found in India and Bangladesh (home to a third of the world's poorest people) but the top 50 MFIs are found in countries as diverse as Morocco, Ecuador, Ethiopia, Serbia, Bosnia and Herzegovina as well as Russia.

The microfinance industry faces challenges. The first is **outreach** – the ability of an MFI to reach poorer and more remote people. Grameen Bank was able to build its success by serving a tightly-knit population and initially requiring groups of borrowers to guarantee loans to their individual members. But while microfinance has achieved a great deal, especially in urban and near-urban areas and with entrepreneurial families, its progress in delivering financial services in less densely populated rural areas has been slow. There are still 3-4 billion people globally who are **unbanked**. Brazil is the success story with 95,000 access points, through post offices, branch networks of big banks and kiosks at petrol stations and shops. Mobile telecoms in parts of Africa are making a big difference.

The second is **sustainability** – the ability of MFIs to cover their costs, in particular the transaction costs of lending very small amounts to very many people. It's an issue faced by all retail commercial banks – the operating costs of maintaining customer accounts. There is a break-even point in providing loans or deposits below which banks lose money on each transaction they make. Poor people usually fall below it and this is compounded amongst thinly-spread rural populations where the cost of a rural branch network is prohibitive.

MFIs survive by charging high rates of interest which can appear abusive, especially when the borrowers are poor. But lending small amounts of money is expensive. Since microloans tend to be for short periods, annualised interest rates may appear high. MFIs argue that they are preferable to moneylenders extorting many times as much. Interest rate ceilings intended to reduce exploitative practices can actually hurt poor people by preventing MFIs from covering their costs, which in turn chokes off the supply of credit.

Funnily enough, those most affected, the **microborrowers** themselves, are least concerned. They prefer to stick with the moneylenders they are familiar with. They are prepared to pay high interest rates for services like quick loan disbursement, confidentiality and flexible repayment schedules.

They don't always see lower interest rates as adequate compensation for having to attend meetings, to undertake training courses to qualify for disbursements, or to make monthly collateral contributions. They also don't like being forced to pretend they are borrowing to start a business, when they often borrow for other reasons (such as school fees, health costs or the family food bill).

Microfinance is attracting a flow of private sector money from institutional investors and has even led to securitisation issues, refinancing microloan portfolios through the bond market. Multilateral agencies (especially parts of the World Bank) have also provided funding to MFIs at below-market rates. The widespread success of the microfinance movement has made the traditional banking industry realise that microcredit borrowers should be more correctly categorised as **pre-bankable**.

Peer-To-Peer Platforms And Crowd-Funding

The slow progress in developing quality savings services for poor people has led to **peer-to-peer platforms** which enable individual lenders in the developed world to provide microloans directly to borrowers (also called **P2P loans**). P2P lenders are also known as **direct or marketplace lenders** and they operate in developed markets too.

Another recent development is **crowd-funding**, allowing small start-ups to raise finance directly from individuals committing small amounts via specialist platforms. Often the investors will be paid partly in product (for instance, chocolate in the case of a confectionery start-up) and the benefit to them is as much to feel involved in the success of a business as for the financial return.

In a further example of how this all connects, both peer-to-peer lending and crowd-funding transactions are increasingly securitised.

Impact Of Technology

These developments in retail finance are technology-enabled. Both peer-to-peer lending and crowd-funding depend on the internet to bring together providers of funding, intermediaries and those seeking it. With microfinance, mobile telephony enables developing economies to overcome the lack of fixed line phone networks to provide financial services directly to individuals. In some countries, the provision of healthcare has been increased by allowing patients to have their transport costs to distant hospitals funded directly via mobile phone payments.

Perhaps surprisingly, the bigger the bank the more it struggles to harness the latest technological advances. This is not through lack of financial resource but rather the impact of **legacy systems**. A legacy system is an older generation of computer. Since banks were amongst the first businesses to computerise they are built on layer upon layer of computerisation. Big banks typically have as many as 4,000 separate systems that don't necessarily intermesh easily.

It's a challenge to make these systems work together apparently seamlessly, while upgrading and replacing them without impacting the retail customer experience. Factor in the challenges for investment banks to keep track of their market positions and you can see how critical – and fragile – the underpinning technology can be. On the retail side perhaps the biggest recent development is mobile banking, which is leading to the scrapping of high street branch networks – provided banks' technology is up to it.

CHAPTER 8

EMERGING MARKETS

Emerging markets – frontier markets – foreign indirect investment – foreign portfolio investment – foreign direct investment – BRICs – Brazil – Russia – India – China – South Africa – MINT – foreign capital – foreign credit – bond market – stock exchanges – privatisations – voucher schemes – import demand – exchange controls – gross domestic product

Under-developed economies are called **emerging markets** or **frontier markets** (the latter tend to be smaller and less developed). They are of interest to banks (for example, specialising in project finance), institutional investors buying shares in local companies (called **foreign indirect investment** or **foreign portfolio investment**) and multinational companies establishing local operations (called **foreign direct investment**). They offer the promise of rapid growth from a low base.

BRICs

Emerging markets shot to prominence in 2001 when Goldman Sachs economist Jim O'Neill gave the collective name **BRICs** to Brazil, Russia, India and China. These are in many respects the antithesis of the tiny, undeveloped, often island, economies that the term 'emerging markets' conjures up. China is already one of the largest economies in the world. India has all of the potential to become one. Russia and Brazil are hardly undeveloped. In any case it's become clear since that the four have little in common with each other.

- **Brazil** has huge natural resources and reserves, is highly developed politically and has a pension fund industry that supports local equity investment. It is dependent on commodity exports (including oil). So it benefited from China's own dramatic growth and the consequent spike in commodity markets globally as China imported raw materials globally. But it has since suffered from China's slowdown.

- **Russia** is the world's second largest oil exporter and benefits alongside the world economy when demand for oil, commodities and natural resources is high. But when the global economy is flat, demand for energy dries up as manufacturers respond to reduced demand by producing less stock. This has a major negative impact on the local stock market, three quarters of which is oil and gas companies. More recently, foreign investors have feared a return to the old ways (including political intervention in neighbouring countries and state expropriation of foreign-owned assets).

- **India** is the least dependent on exports, has a more diversified economy and is less exposed to commodities, making it a more stable long-term prospect. In fact it is now exporting capital overseas. Over recent years Indian companies have made more than 400 acquisitions overseas compared to just 100 each in the case of Russia and China (emerging markets export capital if their own economies lack developed financial markets and savings vehicles). The real challenge for India is whether its fragmented economy will ever operate at full capacity and its markets open up to the beneficial impact of foreign competition.

- **China** is at the forefront of the BRICs. It is the fastest-growing economy in the world and for 20 years grew by almost 10% every year, which meant that output doubled roughly every seven years. Its demand for commodities, such as steel for infrastructure development, drove commodity prices worldwide. However, this growth has slowed significantly, raising fears of recession. China's population is greater than that of the US, the EU and Japan combined – an attractive market for foreign consumer goods companies. But making money in China is hard and many have since retrenched. China accounts for 10% of global output and its position as the world's largest exporter means that China has accumulated the world's largest foreign exchange reserve at $1.7 trillion. Certainly, its sovereign wealth has been used to make several high profile investments overseas in developed markets such as the US and Europe as well as providing direct investment across Africa.

Although they are less of a single economic grouping than the term BRICs suggests, the BRIC countries are trading more with each other and are using each other's currencies to do so, rather than the dollar, with China already providing the de facto reserve currency for Asia and possibly for the BRICs if needed. In 2014 the five BRICS countries (now extended to include South Africa) launched their own development bank in Shanghai (touted as a rival to the World Bank based in the US).

More recently Jim O'Neill has coined the term **MINT** for the next wave of emerging markets: Malaysia, Indonesia, Nigeria and Turkey.

Foreign Credit

The poorest countries survive on foreign aid. Emerging markets move from this to attracting **foreign capital**, for instance in the form of **foreign credit** (foreign banks lending locally, for instance to project finance deals). This may extend to providing credit to the government and local companies.

International banks may help to privatise local state banks by taking stakes in them, which means that banks rather than stock markets play a leading role in funding the local corporate sector. From this a **bond market** may develop, for both government and corporate debt issues.

Stock Market

Many countries see the establishment of a local stock market as a sign that they have arrived financially. After all, a stock market is symbolic of the development of local capital markets. In fact there's a strong argument that emerging markets don't need to have their own stock markets.

The number of **stock exchanges** trebled in the 1990s as many emerging markets, particularly in former central and eastern Europe, launched them. Most started in the wake of **privatisations** of previously state-owned industries in formerly managed economies (for instance, through **voucher schemes**: providing citizens with vouchers with which to buy shares). But liquidity has tended to be thin and new issues sparse. If local companies do list, their shares often end up being traded in the major markets of New York, London and Asia.

A stock market depends on having local institutional investors (insurance companies, pension funds and fund managers) to buy and trade shares. If the participating institutional investors are principally international, there is a real risk that emerging markets can be swamped by an influx of international capital which can just as easily abandon the local market later.

For example, emerging markets were initially less badly affected by the credit crunch because their banks were less exposed to sub-prime instruments and their governments had to spend less on stimulating their economies. But as the credit crunch affected the developed world, foreign capital fled, confidence evaporated, local stock markets plunged and currencies tumbled. The collapse in the credit markets caused havoc as foreign banks stopped lending and offering even basic financial services like trade finance. This global tightening of credit had as much impact as slowing **import demand** in the rich, developed world.

Exchange controls

Emerging markets recovered after the banking crisis through the global loosening of monetary policy. Governments made more money available and reduced interest rates. Cheap capital flowed back into emerging markets. Then as soon the US announced it would be reversing its loosening of monetary policy, foreign capital deserted emerging markets as the prospect of tighter money and higher interest rates pulled it back home.

Some emerging markets impose **exchange controls** for this reason, to stop the volatility of capital inflows and outflows. In these cases international investors can still gain exposure to an emerging market by investing in the shares of multinational companies that are themselves direct investors or whose products are bought locally by a growing middle class of consumers.

In fact it is far from obvious that emerging markets benefit from opening up to global capital. The free-flow of capital across borders should make more funds more cheaply available to poor countries and increased investment should raise local output (**gross domestic product** or **GDP**) and living standards. But economists have not found convincing links between freer capital flows and speedier economic development.

If emerging markets are where the best long-term investment opportunities lie, offshore financial centres are where existing wealth is most concentrated.

CHAPTER 9

OFFSHORE FINANCIAL CENTRES

Shares – bearer – shell companies – bank secrecy – no-tax or low-tax regime – trust law – no investor compensation scheme – financial and professional services infrastructure – OECD – FATF – blacklists – tax information exchange agreements – G20 – cross-border flows – offshore tax loopholes – private banking

We're now beginning to look at where financial institutions and the people who work in them are based. Before looking at the leading international financial centres, of which London is the top, we'll detour via offshore financial centres, so called because many really are offshore: Bermuda, Bahamas, Cayman Islands, the Channel Islands, the Isle of Man, the British Virgin Islands and so on. These days any palm-fringed, sun-baked atoll that hasn't turned itself into an offshore financial centre has really missed a trick. But some aren't islands at all. In fact the most prominent, Switzerland and Liechtenstein, are landlocked.

Brass Plate Companies

Originally many of these were places where you could set up a company, put the **shares** (which were **bearer** anyway so did not appear in any register) in a trust so no one knew who owned them, appoint a shadow board of directors made up of local lawyers and accountants (or even other companies) and open a local bank account with no questions asked and no tax payable, all evidenced by a thin file in a lawyer's office and a brass plate on his wall.

Local trust companies, law firms and accountants prospered mightily on the back of this prosaic business. Some islands – where palm trees outnumbered people – were able to boast tens of thousands of companies with little more than brass plates (**shell companies**) to evidence them and no local industry.

What were all of these companies doing? Holding assets offshore so that mainland tax authorities could not identify and tax them. There was nothing inherently bad or shady about this, although these offshore centres majored on **bank secrecy** so that local banks could promise absolute confidentiality and wouldn't respond to tax inquiries from mainland authorities. Nor should they. It's generally accepted that tax laws don't cross borders and that it is a citizen's right to arrange his affairs to reduce his tax burden so far as he legally can.

Origins

Offshore financial centres thrived because in the main they were former colonial possessions. In return for military protection and tax exemptions provided by the motherland, these island economies were able to forge their own futures without troubling the motherland for continued financial support. How else were they supposed to earn a living?

However, this tolerance of offshore centres – and they were only tolerated because the rich and powerful in mainland economies wanted secret places to stash their wealth – waned when it became clear that organised crime and terrorists were using offshore centres to front funds, and crooked dictators from tinpot republics were creaming off foreign aid into offshore accounts while their people starved.

What offshore financial centres had in common were a number of factors conducive to the secretion of assets, not least the freedom to make their own rules which permitted: (1) a **no-tax or low-tax regime** and a company registry that encouraged businesses with no real local presence to claim legal establishment there while actually operating elsewhere, (2) legal structures based on **trust law** allowing ownership of financial assets to be hidden and (3) bank secrecy laws allowing local banks to conceal the financial details and identities of customers from tax authorities in those countries where those customers were actually based and should be accountable. Two consequences of this were (i) **no investor compensation scheme** to protect against loss through local fraud or corruption – this would have required some sort of local tax or levy and (ii) a **financial and professional services infrastructure** far bigger than the needs of the local economy.

No wonder then, if you were an individual or business with assets you wanted to shield from potential creditors, tax authorities or law enforcement agencies, that you would stick them in an offshore financial centre. A recent World Bank report found that in the 30 years between 1980 and 2010 almost three-quarters of the biggest corruption cases involved shell companies.

Tax: The Central Issue

In 1998 the **OECD** (the Organisation for Economic Co-operation and Development, a club of 30 developed economies) published a seminal paper called *Harmful Tax Competition: An Emerging Global Issue*. At a time when estimates put assets vested in offshore financial centres at over $6 trillion the OECD criticised offshore financial centres for their bank secrecy laws. Since then the inter-governmental Financial Action Task Force (**FATF**) on money laundering and terrorism has taken up the cause. Both the OECD and FATF maintained **blacklists** of offshore financial centres that refused to share information with other countries and would transfer them to white lists as soon as they entered into **tax information exchange agreements** with mainland countries. In 2009 the **G20** (the group of the leading global economies) declared that the era of bank secrecy was over and said it was committed to helping developing countries benefit from a new co-operative tax environment.

Tax is a central issue. The Tax Justice Network has argued for years that tax revenues diverted to offshore financial centres from poor countries would, if retained by those countries, do far more for their development and their people's well-being than all of the developed world's aid programmes put together. Global Financial Integrity, a watchdog, estimates that **cross-border flows** from criminal activity, corruption, capital flight and tax evasion come to over $1 trillion a year, half of which comes from developing markets or transitional markets moving from planned (such as communist) to market (capitalist) economies. Yet aid programmes amount to just $100 billion – a tenth of that – a year.

As attitudes hardened, it became a no-win situation for offshore financial centres. If they didn't reform, they would lose business. Major mainland economies started to close **offshore tax loopholes** (the US for example stopped allowing US companies to use offshore financial centres to avoid tax). But if offshore financial centres reformed too quickly, they would lose businesses to competitors that moved more slowly because they were bigger and could afford to, but had more to lose, such as Liechtenstein and Switzerland.

Offshore Reinvention

The more sophisticated, self-respecting ones have moved with the times. They've renounced bank secrecy laws. They've set up regulatory bodies to vet the quality of the business they attract. They've bowed to pressure from the OECD and others to *share information* and be more *transparent*. And these measures are beginning to work.

Although all offshore financial centres continue to cater for the **private banking** needs of rich individuals, the leading ones have made names for themselves in particular financial niches, such as:

- The establishment of special purpose vehicles (SPVs) as off-the-shelf companies with no assets (shell companies) for *securitisations and repackagings*.

- *Investment management* by offering different fund vehicles for institutional investors.

- *Hedge funds* – Cayman Islands is the capital of the offshore hedge fund industry with over 8,000 registered there accounting for $1 billion in assets (like Bahamas and Bermuda, Cayman benefits from being a quick plane flight away from New York).

- *Reinsurance captives*, that is, offshore reinsurers set up by groups of insurers or reinsurers to enable group members to *self-insure* by keeping the risk (and the premium) within the group, but in a separate offshore entity – especially useful at times when market rates are high.

A number of offshore financial centres have set up stock exchanges to attract multinationals (wishing to add a listing) as well as funds.

Of course, there will always be shady (and not just in the palm trees sense) offshore financial centres out there: the more shady, the less salubrious the customers they attract. Indeed the common joke is that there are some offshore financial centres where you can hide your money so well that even you won't be able to find it again. But in the main offshore financial centres have cleaned up their act to such an extent that they do not even like the term. They resent being called *offshore* financial centres at all and prefer being known as *international* financial centres, like London, New York and so on.

They point out that the Netherlands has for many years encouraged multinationals to put a Dutch holding company at the heart of European operations because of the favourable tax treatment available. And they argue that London too is an offshore financial centre since by some standards it is a low-tax haven, deliberately made so by the UK government to attract and retain wealthy foreigners as residents on the basis that their wealth benefits business and increases employment.

CHAPTER 10

INTERNATIONAL FINANCIAL CENTRES

Muni bond market – invisible earnings – cluster – footfall – reinsurance –
shipping - Lloyd's of London – Baltic Exchange – underwriters –
charterparties – Baltic Exchange Dry Index – primary insurers –
reinsurers – retrocessionaires – underwriting syndicates – managing
agents – Names – members' agents – brokers – slip – working Names –
corporate Names – alternative risk transfer (ART) – annual contract –
premium – multi-year insurance contract – catastrophe bonds – standby
facility – letter of credit – securitise – on line – excess – reference event –
loss tranches – weather derivatives

Offshore financial centres are tiny compared to the world's leading international financial centres. Here a distinction has to be drawn between the world's largest economies and where the financial markets we've been discussing take place. The US, China and Japan are the world's biggest economies. But more securities (shares and bonds) and other financial instruments and transactions are traded or undertaken in London than anywhere else.

As a rough rule-of-thumb, if the US is the most highly capitalised market at about $20 trillion, then China would follow (about $7 trillion), Japan (about $5 trillion), then Germany, the UK and France (about 3 each), India, Russia and Brazil (1 to 2), Australia, Switzerland and Hong Kong (about 1 each). In terms of the comparative size of international financial centres, if New York was a 140-storey skyscraper, Tokyo would follow (40 storeys), then London (30), then France and Germany (10 each), Canada (8), Hong and Switzerland (5 each), Spain and Australia (4 each), Taiwan (3) followed by Sweden, South Korea and Finland (2 each).

Size Of Domestic Markets

New York and Tokyo are bigger than London as markets because they have much larger domestic economies which provide a financial hinterland (with China obviously catching up fast). For example, US municipalities (towns and cities) borrow money by issuing bonds entirely within the US. The US **muni bond market** is in its own right one of the largest financial markets in the world. So, despite the emergence of China and India, the US is still the single biggest economy in the world. The US has the biggest domestic financial markets in the world too, and it's their size which gives the US its international dominance, along with the fact that, as the world's biggest economy, its currency is also the world's reserve currency.

Japan has massive domestic financial markets too – its Post Office, which is where most ordinary Japanese park their savings, is the single biggest investment institution in the world. But whereas New York is outward-looking across the rest of the US and the world, Tokyo is inward-looking and reflects Japan's historically introverted and isolated outlook. Tokyo almost rivalled New York in the 1980s. But the Japanese economy fell back in the 1990s and with it so did Tokyo's position as an international financial centre. This is why London, despite its much smaller economy, is actually the leading *international* financial centre – more of the international financial markets take place in London than anywhere else, and the provision of financial services internationally is a significant contributor to the UK's economy.

These three – New York, Tokyo and London – dwarf the others. In the international financial markets, size matters. The bigger the market, the more liquid and efficient it is: the more securities on offer, the more buyers and sellers, the easier and cheaper it is to trade, and the greater the possible volumes. The biggest markets attract the most customers. It becomes self-perpetuating. Those three are unlikely to be rivalled for at least another decade or two and then it will be by Shanghai in conjunction with Hong Kong. The two markets have pioneered a link called Stock Connect that allows international investors to buy Chinese shares without requiring government approval for each individual purchase, the first time Chinese markets have opened up.

Why London Is Top

London is to finance as Wimbledon is to tennis. The top international players want to be there. A number of reasons are given for London's pre-eminence, from its flexible regulatory and tax systems that are particularly welcoming to foreign financiers, down to the pleasantness of London as a place to house your family. But the truth is more mundane: luck and history.

London is the top international financial centre for the same reason that English is (still) the language of international business (itself a reason): Britain's trading history. It also helps that the UK is in Europe's time zone, handily placed between Asia and the US. The Brits also spotted the importance of the City's **invisible earnings** (as they are called) to the country's economy some decades ago and have since done everything possible to maintain its position.

The City has its own government (the City of London Corporation), mayor and police service and it is a geographical place in its own right (known as the Square Mile). One of the City of London Corporation's key roles is marketing the City to the rest of the financial world. The infrastructure that has accreted around London's financial markets over the centuries is deep and hard to replicate or topple.

The City is what economists call a **cluster**. People come to do business there because everybody else is there, competitors included. If you are a carpet salesman, economists will tell you that you will get more business setting up shop in Carpet Street alongside competitors than if you decide to set up somewhere else far away from them. This is because people who are serious about buying a carpet will come to Carpet Street and you will benefit from the greater **footfall** (passing traffic of likely customers).

So with the City. In fact there are streets whose names indicate that centuries ago they were clusters in their own right – Bread Street, Milk Street, Wood Street – and (as mentioned earlier) Lombard Street is where the bankers from Lombardy who came over from northern Italy in the middle ages set up shop. The very first bankers were goldsmiths, who lent out the gold that was deposited with them for safe-keeping, and there is still a goldsmiths' livery company.

History

This history has a direct impact on today's markets. It explains why more bonds and derivatives are traded in London than anywhere else – contributing to $500 billion in daily turnover. There are more banks (several hundred) than anywhere else. More than half of Europe's equity investment ($5.5 trillion) is managed in London (funds under management are greater than those of the next 10 European centres put together). Three quarters of European hedge fund assets are run from London. London dominates commodity markets: 95% of the world's trading in aluminium, copper, lead, nickel, silver, tin and zinc is conducted from London.

Most of the markets are virtual. They exist in space as trades between market participants carried out on screen, by email and over the phone. The London Stock Exchange became a virtual market over thirty years ago. The way it works in practice is that when a member of the exchange (an intermediary such as a broker) carries out a trade in a share listed on the stock exchange, it has to send information about that trade (which share, how many, what price) to the exchange which immediately publishes that data to all other members. In this way everyone knows the current state of the market – the last trade and its price.

Bricks And Clicks

Something else flows from this. There are few barriers these days to flows of money around the world. True, some smaller countries try to stop foreign money swirling into and out of their domestic markets because they would be swamped. But on the whole money in the financial markets is like water: it flows to where the returns are greatest.

Think of the international financial markets as taking place virtually in the air around you – up in the sky. But the people who work in them, for issuers, intermediaries and investors, are not virtual. They are on the ground. They work in international financial centres such as London. Without them the international financial markets wouldn't happen. So the financial markets are a bit like computer clicks. And the financial centres are the bricks.

You can begin to see that the City is really lots of different markets. People come to the City because they want to buy or sell and they know there will be other people there they can trade with – like any market, a car-boot sale or eBay.

Shipping And Insurance

The City is home to other key global markets that, strictly speaking, are not financial but are linked symbiotically to the financial markets we've discussed. These are the global **reinsurance** market and the **shipping** market.

The reinsurance market is called **Lloyd's of London** (which has nothing to do with the banking group of similar name). It's headquartered at the eastern end of the City, the part that's historically and geographically closest to London's old docks. The shipping market is called the **Baltic Exchange** from London's maritime trading links centuries ago with the Hanseatic League city states like Hamburg on the Baltic Sea. Insurance and shipping are intimately connected. The one was spawned by the other: people with maritime interests – captains, shipowners and merchants with cargoes – would gather in Edward Lloyd's coffee shop in the 1690s to make deals and share information about the fates of vessels and their cargoes.

Wealthy individuals would share the risk of insuring a ship and its cargo and became known as **underwriters**. They had unlimited liability, meaning they had to meet a claim in full even if it bankrupted them. Eventually the insurance market outgrew the coffee shop and moved, taking the name with it, while the buying and selling of cargo carrying capacity (called **charterparties**) became the Baltic Exchange.

This is still the case today: the **Baltic Exchange Dry Index** is the world's leading barometer of the shipping market and therefore of the global economy. Four-fifths of the world's goods are transported by ship so if the Dry Index moves up it means that global production is increasing as exporters book more space on ships to fulfil orders.

From marine risk (still half of Lloyd's of London's business) underwriters diversified. Lloyd's is not strictly an insurance market but a **reinsurance** market. **Primary insurers** (insurance companies) take on risk then lay it off to **reinsurers** (which often have the word Re in their name, as in Swiss Re, and are also known as **retrocessionaires**) and so to Lloyd's. Every major global risk ends up at Lloyd's sooner or later. Lloyd's is therefore the leading market for the pricing of risk and any new risk (movie stars in the 1930s, satellites in the 1970s, terrorism more recently) is calibrated first at Lloyd's. This is its expertise.

The market's structure reflects its history: risk is taken on by **underwriting syndicates** run by **managing agents**. The underwriting capacity is provided by investors called **Names** (always written with an initial capital) whose interests are served by **members' agents** who put them on syndicates that reflect their risk/reward appetite. **Brokers** bring risks to the market on behalf of clients and get those risks underwritten by one or more syndicates (which note their share of the risk on the **slip** as it's called). Names used to be actual individuals. But a perfect storm in the 1990s of (a) massive global disasters, (b) longtail asbestosis liability from decades before, (c) a market structure that favoured the interests of **working Names** (Names who were also managing agents of syndicates) and (d) pure fraud, all led to the market being gridlocked by litigation. This was resolved by hiving off existing risks into a reserve vehicle called Equitas, phasing out individual Names (many of whom had gone bankrupt) and starting again.

It was a traumatic period that almost brought Lloyd's of London to its knees. But, throughout, it never failed to meet a claim (it never has; if it did, Lloyd's would never recover). Now the underwriting capacity is provided by **corporate Names** which are like investment funds. The history of the market lives on: the Lutine bell (from the wreck of the ship of that name) is still rung when a disaster occurs leading to a claim at Lloyd's.

Alternative Risk Transfer

Two key financial products have resulted from interplay between the insurance and capital markets. One is **alternative risk transfer** (**ART**). Let's say a fictitious oil exploration company (let's call it Exoil) has several drilling rigs in the North Sea. It insures them. But insurance is an **annual contract**: Exoil pays a **premium** each year. If no claim arises that premium is lost. But Exoil knows that it loses an oil rig through a disaster on average once every 10 years. ART is like a **multi-year insurance contract**. It treats the premium more as a saving pot towards the cost of replacing a rig. Exoil gets some of the annual premium rebated if it has no claims that year. But if a rig does sink, the insurer doesn't meet the entire cost. Rather it may meet some of the cost and provide cheap financing for the rest at the very time when Exoil would find raising money in the financial markets expensive (because, having just lost a rig, its profitability is at risk and the business is impaired). Insurance here is more of a cross between financing and asset replacement and the premium rebates in good years make it cheaper for Exoil than conventional insurance.

Catastrophe Bonds

The other product is even more extreme: **catastrophe bonds** (known as cat bonds). But it works the same way, more like a **standby facility** (an overdraft) or a **letter of credit**. At its simplest, you take a risk of a catastrophe (say a hurricane or an earthquake) and you **securitise** it by turning it into a bond. In other words, an insurance company insures the risk then buys a reinsurance contract from an SPV (special purpose vehicle) which issues catastrophe bonds to institutional investors. The bond, as usual, has a specified maturity, which can be anything from short- to long-term. Now, this is where it gets interesting. If, during the life of the bond, the catastrophe occurs, the investors lose interest on the bond for a period and even part of their principal – depending on the terms of the bond. Yet cat bonds have found buyers, especially amongst hedge funds (surprise, surprise).

To understand this, you have to understand how insurance works. Essentially, insurers offer cover in layers. So, for a catastrophe, the first layer might be $1 billion: any losses up to $1 billion are within that layer and met by the insurer or insurers **on line** for that layer. But if the losses spike up through that layer, then any **excess** which pushes the losses into the next layer is met by the insurers of the next layer. So, as a pension fund, you might buy a bond that is only at risk if losses hit more than, say, $10 billion. Now, that would require a heck of a catastrophe, so in the context of risk, it's not such a gamble as it may sound. A more sophisticated version may make the trigger not so much the catastrophe itself but a **reference event** such as the level of the insurance company's own loss; or the level of industry losses. And the bond may be structured not only in **loss tranches** (as above) but in terms of whether the bondholder loses principal or simply forgoes interest and recovers the principal at the end of the bond's term. This provides the insured with an interest-free loan for a given period (the life of the bond) to give it time (and the funds) to recover.

If so, the investor is actually doing nothing more foolish than making an interest-free loan which is exactly what is required when a catastrophe occurs: money to put things right that in due course can be paid back or refinanced; at a point when (like Exoil) money may be otherwise difficult to raise. Of course, if the trigger event doesn't happen, the investor pockets a high rate of interest to reward it for the risk. The very first cat bond was due to be issued by the California Earthquake Authority in 1995. It never happened. Effectively, Warren Buffett, the world's most successful investor, bought the whole thing. Over the period insured there weren't any earthquakes. Presumably he made a mint. Similar techniques lie behind **weather derivatives** that protect holiday companies that want good weather and energy companies that want bad (so that people use more heating).

The benefit of both of these is that capital markets' capacity (roughly $20 trillion) is used to top-up reinsurance capacity (roughly $150 billion) and the risk is spread more widely amongst investors than it might have been if it had remained concentrated in the insurance and reinsurance markets.

Talk of insurance brings us back to where we started: institutional investors. We've looked at what the international financial markets are. We've looked at the international financial centres where they take place. Along the way we've mentioned the participants – institutional investors, intermediaries and issuers. Now it's time to look at them in more detail.

CHAPTER 11

MARKET PARTICIPANTS

Institutional investors – intermediaries – issuers – buy side – sell side – insurance companies – pension funds – defined benefits – defined contributions – asset class – asset allocation – upper quartile – benchmarked – churn – shareholder activism – index-tracking – passive management – beta – alpha – smart beta – collective investment schemes – unit trust – mutual funds – open-ended – investment trust – closed-ended – hedge funds – sovereign wealth funds – random walk – value investing – spread – soft commissions – prime brokerage – custody – corporate finance – takeovers (M&A) – venture capital – private equity – alternative asset managers

I started this book by mentioning the three types of market participant: **institutional investors**; **intermediaries**; and **issuers**. Now you know all about the financial markets in which they operate we can go back to each of these and take a closer look at what they actually do.

1   INSTITUTIONAL INVESTORS

Institutional investors fall into three types: insurance companies, pension funds and investment management companies (also known as fund managers). In the markets they are known collectively as **buy side** because they buy securities (shares and bonds) from the **sell side** (issuers and the intermediaries).

Insurance Companies

We pay **insurance companies** premiums in return for two types of insurance: casualty insurance and life assurance. Insurance companies used to do one or the other. Now the big ones (called *composites*) do both.

Casualty insurance provides cover against financial loss and loss of possessions. Examples include household insurance, car insurance and holiday insurance (*casualty* here is what you and I would call *accident*). These are what people generally mean when talking about insurance.

Life assurance is a bit different. It provides insurance against death. Now, whereas a casualty may not occur, death is *assured* (certain) so this kind of insurance is really about using premiums to build up a pot of money so that when you die your dependants (such as family members) have something to live on.

Where life and casualty meet is in providing insurance against long-term illness or disability. This is often part of a life assurance package, so that if you can't carry on working the policy kicks in and gives you an income to live on. It protects you against the possibility (casualty) of long-term illness or disability.

The key aspect of insurance companies is that they don't – as is popularly thought – make a profit by paying out less in claims than they receive in premium income. In fact it's by investing the premium income in the markets that they are able to generate a return that allows them to meet claims and make a profit. So insurers have two sides to their business: risk assessment; and investment management.

Outside the world's main financial centres there are cities where insurance companies are concentrated: Hartford, Connecticut in the US is one; Zurich in Switzerland another.

Pension Funds

Pension provision works on a similar basis to life assurance: you set aside money during your working life to pay for your retirement. Some insurers provide pension products too.

Pension funds (also called pension schemes or plans) are attached to sponsoring companies (sponsors) and invest over the long term to provide the company's employees with pensions when they retire. In many schemes the employer will match the employee's monthly contribution made out of his or her salary. Pension contributions often attract tax relief – government likes encouraging people to provide for their future, otherwise it has to.

Pensions used to be generous. Often you would retire on two-thirds of your final salary. Since you were likely to be senior and at your highest earning level when you retired this provided you with a good income. By then you'd probably paid off the mortgage and seen your children through education. This type of pension was called **defined benefits**. You knew what you would be getting because the *benefits* (what you would be getting) were *defined* (specified at the outset).

Very few pension schemes are like this now. People live much longer (so their retirement costs more) and changes in regulation have meant that pension schemes have to account much more precisely for their future liabilities (to future pensioners) and how they will meet them. So defined benefits have become too expensive to sustain. Instead pension schemes have been switching to **defined contributions**. This means you know how much (*defined*) you have to pay in (*contribution*): but what it will provide when you retire is anyone's guess. In short the pension scheme builds up a pot of money for you over the course of your employment and then when you retire you use that pot of money to buy an annuity.

An annuity is, in theory, a contract that pays you a fixed amount of money every year (an annual amount, hence the name – calculated on a yearly basis but in fact paid monthly like a salary). The principal providers of annuities are insurance companies – another reason why they are investment machines. Because defined contribution schemes enable you to buy an annuity they are also called money purchase schemes.

Of course, nowadays, people move around jobs a lot more often and many more work for themselves. So personal pensions, where you look after your own financial future, are more common.

The relationship between a pension fund and its host, the sponsoring company, can be tense. In the UK each pension fund is set up as a trust with a board of trustees comprising representatives from amongst the employees as well as the employer (often the company's finance director is the chair of trustees). The employer wants to keep its contributions to a minimum because they reduce its profit. Whenever a pension fund is *fully funded* (it has enough by way of assets to meet its future liabilities) the sponsor may take what's called a *contributions holiday*: it suspends making any contributions to the fund itself. Increasingly pension funds find they are not fully funded as people live longer, and investment returns can be very up and down (especially given the financial crises of the last two decades). So they may seek more from the sponsor.

Unfunded Pension Liabilities

This is in contrast to most public-sector pensions which are *unfunded*, that is, they are paid out of current tax receipts. They too have started to change in that the benefits they pay are being reduced. Traditionally public sector employees didn't earn much but were rewarded in retirement with good pensions. Over the last few years, however, the salaries of some public sector employees, such as the chief executives of local authorities, have soared so this argument has become harder to justify.

In other parts of Europe the tradition has been for pensions to be unfunded so they face more of a *demographic time bomb*, where an ageing population means that in due course more people will be in retirement than in work with the latter effectively supporting the former through taxes. The country likely to be hardest hit in this way by an ageing population is Japan.

A pension fund will use a number of consultants, including an *actuary*. Actuaries are statisticians who can work out the incidence of fatality from the lifestyle profiles of a group of people big enough to be an effective sample. If I asked an actuary at what age I was likely to die, they wouldn't know: they're not a soothsayer. If I gave an actuary a profile of a group of five hundred people (gender split, ages, type of employment, how many smoked, how many drank, how many exercise regularly, and so on) they would be able to tell me what percentage of the sample would die at what age. This is how pension funds work out their future liabilities (in other words how many pensioners will live to what age) so that they know how much they need to invest and what return they need to generate.

Other consultants (often part of the same actuarial firm) will advise on which external fund managers to use, will help in their selection and will monitor their performance. This is because only the biggest pension funds attached to the most established companies have sufficient assets to manage their money themselves. They will employ *in-house fund managers*. Even so they will put some of their assets out to *external fund managers* and the investment management arms of insurers to run. This is both to keep their own fund managers on their toes but also to get the benefit of specialist investment expertise.

Asset Classes

This is because fund managers specialise. Broadly they specialise by what is called **asset class**. We've covered many of the asset classes already: shares (known as equities by fund managers), bonds (fixed income), currencies and derivatives, commodities (such as oil and gold) as well as cash. Each of these is a different asset class.

Another is commercial property (also known as real estate) such as offices, factories, warehouses, shops and shopping malls, forests and farmland). Investment is either direct (by buying and developing commercial property) or indirect by investing in real estate companies and real estate funds (called REITs – real estate investment trusts).

Major institutional investors will invest in all of these and do so globally, around the world in different markets. They do this to maximise their investment return while minimising the risk – by ensuring they keep their eggs in as many baskets as possible, which is known as diversifying your portfolio.

In fact the real impact on an institutional investor's portfolio performance is driven by what percentage of its assets it invests in the different available asset classes rather than the individual performance of each. This decision – of how to allocate your assets is called **asset allocation** and is driven by things like: where you are based (so which currency you should be exposed to); your liabilities and how long- or short-term (a pension fund with immediate liabilities should be switching from equities to bonds) and so on. Often external consultants will also help with asset allocation.

Investment Performance

Many pension funds don't have any in-house fund managers themselves. Instead they put all of their assets out to external fund managers to manage. Others, smaller still, may park their portfolio with an insurer for it to run on a *segregated* basis (where their assets are managed separately from others) or *pooled* with those of other pension funds and managed collectively (which is cheaper).

Fund managers are judged on a quarterly basis. Every three months the trustees will meet with their external managers and consultants. For the fund managers the quest is to be **upper quartile**, which means in the top 25 per cent of fund managers in their specialisation. This is necessarily a *zero-sum game*, that's to say, for everyone who is upper quartile there must be an equivalent in the bottom quartile since the universe of managers is **benchmarked** against the average. What is odd about all this is that most institutional investors will stress the importance of *long-term performance* yet judge their managers on a shorter timescale. If your performance lags the market you will lose your mandate (be fired).

This can lead to two unfortunate side-effects. One is called **churn** where a manager starts to buy and sell frantically in the hope of finding the right combination of investments to lift his or her performance. Churning a portfolio is expensive because every time you buy and sell there are transactional costs of using a broker and getting in and out of the market.

The other is an emphasis on *short-term performance* which occasionally afflicts the City, where pension funds berate their managers for poor short-term performance so managers become short-term in their investment outlook and berate the companies they invest in for not producing short-term profit improvements. A constant complaint is that institutional shareholders do not hold managements to account. It's easier just to sell the shares. This is changing with long-term shareholders engaging more with the companies they invest in. This is called **shareholder activism**. Hedge funds can take it to extremes, pressurising companies they invest in to sell assets to realise value.

Index-Tracking (Passive Investment)

Increasingly institutional investors are aware that benchmarking fund managers against an index (an average) means the average fund manager is only as good as the index but, adding in costs, underperforms it. Since few fund managers consistently outperform, institutional investors are better off *owning the index*. In other words, if you want to track the FTSE 100, simply buy a share in every one of the hundred companies that make up the FTSE 100: that way, when it goes up, you go up. This is called **index-tracking**. Now, you don't need an expensive money manager doing the stock selection for you. In fact you don't need anyone doing it at all: you can program a computer to do it, which is why it is also called **passive management** (unlike using actual money managers who decide what to invest in, which is called *active management*). Nor do you need to buy all one hundred constituent shares. You can *sample*, that is, buy enough to approximate the index.

There are some shares that follow the market almost precisely (they are said to have a **beta** of one where beta is the measure of how closely a share *correlates* to the market to which it belongs). Shares with a beta of one follow the index up and down precisely and are used to create a sample index. Many institutional investors will have their *core portfolio* invested passively and then have active management around the periphery, adding (they hope) above-market additional performance (called **alpha**). **Smart beta** funds follow customised indices that are more focused than standard indices (which are dominated by the largest companies).

The difference in fees between passive and active can be significant. An active manager will charge anything from one to three per cent of *assets under management* (*a.u.m.*) whereas index tracking can cost as little as 0.05% – this is because it can be done by computer. Of course you now know that you don't even need to buy shares: you can buy a stock index future instead and with a single contract get synthetic exposure to the underlying index.

Investment Management Companies

These fund managers I've been referring to may work for insurance companies and pension funds. Or they may work in investment management companies. Investment management companies are in fact the third type of institutional investor (after insurance companies and pension funds). They are known as fund managers, money managers, asset managers, wealth managers, investment managers and portfolio managers. All mean the same thing. Some are public, listed companies. Some are private, owned by those who set them up and work in them. Some are owned by banks or insurance companies. Apart from the world's top financial centres, cities which have big concentrations of fund managers include Boston, Edinburgh, Geneva and Singapore, as well as some tax havens.

They manage *retail* money for people who are individual clients and *wholesale* (meaning business-to-business) money for insurance companies and pension funds. Most investment management companies have a mix of both. People who are rich enough (high-net-worths) may have a fund manager or broker to manage their personal portfolio on a *discretionary* basis (the fund manager decides what and when to buy or sell) or on an *advisory* basis (the manager advises the client who takes the ultimate decision). Investment management companies are called fund managers because the bulk of the money they manage is in **collective investment schemes**, also known as pooled investments or funds. Individuals buy shares or units in a fund and the fund manager invests that money in the markets on their behalf.

Open the personal finance pages of any national newspaper and you will see the array of funds on offer. Most funds invest in equities. But there are many bond funds (these provide steady income but little capital growth because they invest in fixed-interest instruments; good for pensioners). There are *balanced* funds that invest in both. There are currency funds, commodity funds (such as gold) and property funds (investing in commercial property). Equity funds fall broadly into the following categories:

- *Growth* – these funds specialise in identifying shares that will provide capital growth over the medium- to long-term; income from dividends is not a priority. They invest in companies that will grow faster in capital value than the market average which may mean that they don't pay out much by way of dividend (putting any profits back into growth).

- *Income* – these funds invest in shares with strong dividend flows and in bonds; these may be companies in mature industries that may not grow much but which pay steady dividends. They are favoured by investors needing regular income, such as pensioners. Ironically, shares that provide steady dividend flows tend to be attractive and therefore go up in value, so that income funds can provide good growth as well. Growth and income shares may also be classified as *defensives* (good in downturns) and *cyclicals* (exposed to economic ups and downs).

- *Small-cap / Mid-cap* – whereas the above funds tend to focus on large UK companies (the biggest shares are known as 'blue chip') small-cap ('cap' stands for capitalisation) and mid-cap funds focus on smaller listed companies where growth may be greater but so is the risk of a company going bust. Some are called 'penny shares' because their shares are worth only a few pence. But if you buy into a company whose shares are trading at 4p and they go up to 8p, you have doubled your money.

- *VCTs* – these are *venture capital trusts* that invest in unlisted start-ups and young businesses. They are high-risk, aimed at sophisticated investors, and offer tax allowances that are attractive to the wealthy.

- *Index* – index funds simply track an index such as the FTSE 100, 250 or All-Share; they do so by sampling (holding representative shares) or holding every share or through derivatives; the idea is that they provide an average performance year-in, year-out whereas active funds (all the other ones mentioned here are active funds) may underperform the index more often than they outperform it.

- *Sector-specific* – these funds restrict themselves to a sector such as telecoms, technology, financials and are for investors who want exposure to a particular industry.

- *Region-specific* – these funds focus on markets outside the UK, such as mainland Europe, North America, Asia and emerging markets. The term 'ex' means excluding, so Europe ex-UK means Europe excluding the UK, Asia ex-Japan means investing in Asia but not Japan (because there are many country-specific funds providing that exposure).

- *International* – these funds invest outside the home country in whichever markets seem attractive at the time (they often have a growth or income emphasis); whereas *global* funds can also invest in the domestic market too.

Types Of Fund Structure

The actual fund vehicles fall into three types.

The most common is the **unit trust**, so called because the legal structure is a trust and it issues units (known as **mutual funds** in the US). Investors buy units from the fund manager who runs it. Let's say I launch a unit trust and because I am known in the market I get a hundred investors. They each buy a unit at, let's say, £1 each. That means I have £100 to invest. I invest successfully and after a while those initial investments are worth £150.

Let's say you are a *unit holder* and decide to sell. You come to me with your unit. I *redeem* (cancel) it and give you £1.50 (value of the fund divided by the number of units in issue – to keep it simple I'm ignoring the costs of running the fund and my fees). Now if at that point a new investor appears I would issue them with one or more units at £1.50 because that is now what a unit in the fund costs. In fact it doesn't matter how many units they want provided they can pay £1.50 for each one. For this reason unit trusts are called **open-ended** because the fund manager can issue as many units as there are investors prepared to pay for them.

In fact fund managers want to attract more money to invest because their fees (a reflection of assets under management) go up accordingly. But in truth fund managers don't want their funds getting too big: the bigger the fund the harder to move in and out of markets efficiently and the harder to find investment opportunities that will make a real difference to the fund's overall return.

Unit trusts are not ideal for illiquid markets (such as venture capital, emerging markets or property). This is because when an investor wants to exit, the fund manager has to liquidate investments to meet the redemption (or keep enough cash to do so). It's also an issue in volatile markets. If investors get spooked and rush to redeem, the fund manager will have to sell his or her best investments (in a falling market they will realise the best price and will be easier to sell) to raise the needed cash.

Investment Trusts / Investment Companies

A better vehicle for illiquid markets is the **investment trust**. Originally this too was, legally speaking, a trust. Nowadays they are public listed companies (and tend to be called *investment companies*). They were dreamt up in the 1860s by Scottish lawyers in Edinburgh who wanted a safe place for their wealthy clients to invest. Investment trusts invest in the shares of several hundred other public companies. This provides much greater diversification for investors who may only be able to afford to buy a few shares: better in an investment trust than one or two companies.

Because an investment trust is just a public listed company, investors buy shares in it through the stock exchange, not by going to the fund manager. This is a critical distinction from a unit trust.

It means that how much the fund manager has to invest does not depend on whether investors are buying or selling shares. The investment trust will have raised an initial amount to invest when it floated and can raise more through a rights issue, but otherwise the funds at its disposal to invest are not affected by the trust's own share price and whether people are buying or selling shares in it. Hence the advantage for illiquid markets and the reason why investment trusts are called **closed-ended** (the fund manager cannot issue additional shares at will so there is always a finite number in issue).

Investment trusts are good vehicles for income investors because, as companies, they do not have to pay out all of their income and can use reserves to smooth out dividend payments from year to year. This has enabled some investment trusts to achieve an unbroken and rising annual dividend for decades.

Also, as companies, they are able to borrow. This gearing is good when markets are rising because it increases their market exposure (provided the increased return is greater than the cost of borrowing). But it can accentuate market falls (bigger market exposure to falling prices plus the cost of borrowing).

Investment trusts have become more popular in recent years because in the past financial advisers were paid commission by unit trusts for recommending them. Investment trusts as public companies couldn't do this. But following the RDR (the Retail Distribution Review) in the UK in recent years, commission payments have been banned, leading to a more level playing field.

One quirk of investment trusts is that their share price may depart from the value of their underlying investments. Trusts seen to have good managers may see their shares rise to a *premium* over the *net asset value* ('net', because any borrowings are stripped out when arriving at the value of the underlying investments). Some may trade at a *discount*, which undervalues the trust and its management team.

Many have therefore adopted a *discount control mechanism* (known as a DCM) which allows them to buy in their own shares when they fall to a discount (so narrowing the discount) and issue fresh shares when they are at a premium (reducing the premium). In this way the share price is brought closer in line with the net asset value.

Real Estate Investment Trusts (REITs)

A specialist type of investment trust is the REIT (real estate investment trust – pronounced 'reet') which was established in the US in 1960. REITs are public listed companies that specialise in buying and holding commercial property (offices, factories, shopping malls). In the US they hold 20% of all commercial property assets and have a combined capitalisation of half a billion dollars.

Here the investment trust makes access to the underlying investment more liquid. The problem with property is that it takes time to buy and sell, often up to six months from first viewing to completion. By interposing a REIT investors are able to trade in and out of commercial property simply by dealing in the REIT's shares, without dealing in or disturbing the underlying investment.

The third type of fund is a bit of both: it's a company but is open-ended and is called an OEIC (pronounced 'oik') which stands for open-ended investment company.

Other investment vehicles include the limited liability partnership or LLP. These are favoured by pension funds because they are transparent for tax purposes (they don't increase the tax charged).

LLPs are often used for private equity funds. These are funds set up by investment banks and specialist buy-out houses that raise capital from institutional investors in order to buy public companies (through takeovers and M&A deals – mergers and acquisitions), break them up and sell off the component businesses for more than the company itself cost, so releasing value. These deals are often called *public-to-private* deals. If a lot of debt is used in the takeover it is called a *leveraged buy-out* (*LBO*).

Other Types Of Fund

A *fund-of-funds* is a fund that invests in other funds (a variation is the *multi-manager fund*). It does this in order to pick those funds that are outperforming the rest and will switch its investments between funds accordingly. The only disadvantage is the double level of fees – one set of fees to the manager of the fund-of-funds, the other set to the funds it invests in.

Exchange traded funds are passive funds that track an index but, like investment trusts, are traded on a stock exchange. This means they experience price changes on a minute-by-minute basis throughout the trading day as they are bought and sold (whereas a unit trust is priced once a day after the underlying share values have been totalled). This makes ETFs particularly responsive to intra-day price changes in the market which is why they are popular with *day traders* (retail investors who trade online and hope to make money over the course of the day, close out their positions at the end of the day and start again the next).

Unlike trackers which follow broad indices, ETFs can be based on customised baskets of securities (for instance, just mining shares). However, some ETFs are synthetic: they don't invest in the index; instead the fund manager enters into a swap with a bank which pays up if the index goes up. This adds counterparty risk (of the bank defaulting). ETFs enable investors to get immediate exposure to a market without stock picking. But, although they are passive funds, they encourage trading whereas index funds traditionally are designed to be buy-and-hold long-term investment vehicles.

Hedge Funds

Hedge funds are institutional investors in their own right. They attract money from pension funds, insurance companies and high-net-worths (rich people) and use it to buy derivatives. Hedging is the use of derivatives to mitigate (minimise) risk. But hedge funds don't use derivatives to hedge but (by buying on margin and exploiting derivatives' natural gearing effect) to command much bigger positions than they could simply by investing in the underlying instruments. In other words, to make big bets on market movements.

They also *short* the market. Traditional funds are called *long funds* because they make investments in the expectation that whatever they buy will go up. Buying anything in the markets is called going long of it. But, as we've seen, the financial markets are places where you can sell something you don't actually own in the hope of being able to buy it more cheaply later (shorting or going short). You do this where you think it will go down in value: you sell it high, buy it cheap and your profit is the difference. On the date when the trade settles you borrow the securities in question to settle the trade then buy them back in the market to return to the lender (stock lending, mentioned earlier). Long-short hedge funds, for example, buy shares they consider undervalued and short those they consider overvalued.

Hedge funds can also be highly leveraged (borrowing heavily to back their positions) which, when taken with the gearing effect of derivatives, can amplify their market position to the extent that hedge funds can drive market movements just through their own activity.

All of this makes hedge funds highly volatile and risky investment vehicles. Investors won't put more than a small percentage of their portfolio into hedge funds because they might lose the lot. But hedge funds can deliver spectacular performance. In their heyday they could generate returns of 40% – until everyone tried to do the same, the market became too crowded and those opportunities disappeared.

So institutional investors use them to add performance spice to the peripheries of their portfolios.

Hedge funds don't benchmark themselves against indices. Instead they aim for absolute returns (making as much money as possible). In return, hedge fund managers expect to be paid high performance fees. The norm is *two-and-twenty* meaning two per cent of assets under management (the standard active management charge) plus 20 per cent of any increase in value. To generate these sorts of returns they often take high-risk stakes in illiquid positions that are hard to unwind (such as a privately-owned gold mining company) and for this reason they may lock in investors for as long as five years. Investors who want to get out early may seek a buyer of their stake so there is an active secondary market in hedge fund participations.

Hedge funds are high-risk, high-reward vehicles. Some are run by *quants* (quantitative analysts – usually ex-scientists) who use algorithms to spot market anomalies. Others are *macro funds*, seeking to exploit long-term secular trends.

Many have gone bust, most spectacularly Long-Term Capital Management in 1998 which lost $4 billion and had gearing of 50:1 ($50 borrowed for every $1 invested in it). Given the risks of choosing the wrong hedge fund, fund-of-fund structures have been a popular conduit to invest in hedge funds, in order to spread the risk.

Sovereign Wealth Funds

Sovereign wealth funds (SWFs) are amongst the largest institutional investors. They are state-controlled investment funds that channel a country's surplus income – from natural resources such as oil and gas or else from overseas trade and exports – into assets overseas for the benefit of future generations. The idea of SWFs has been around for 50 years although only recently have they begun to attract much attention. One of the first belonged to the Pacific island of Nauru which built up (and lost) a fund of several hundred million dollars from of its phosphate exports of seabird droppings. Another is the Kuwait Investment Authority (and its overseas sibling, the Kuwait Investment Office) which also started in the 1950s. The biggest is the Abu Dhabi Investment Authority (roughly a trillion dollars). China's is variously reported to be the biggest or to have just $200 billion in assets. Total assets of SWFs are estimated at about $3 trillion.

What's surprising is just how many countries have them, from the State Oil Fund of the Republic of Azerbaijan to Venezuela's Investment Fund for Macroeconomic Stabilisation. An interesting contrast in fortunes is that between Norway, which put the revenues from North Sea oil into an SWF and the UK which didn't. Norway's SWF is now worth about $400 billion.

Most striking is how many of these funds are from emerging markets. Apart from Norway, Australia's Future Fund and Canada's Alberta Heritage Savings Trust Fund are amongst the few SWFs from developed economies. And therein lies the political issue. Developed economies, advocates for years of free and open international financial markets, don't like it when these SWFs sweep in and buy up swathes of their own economies – especially when they're from China and Russia.

SWFs have responded by forming bodies (such as the Sovereign Wealth Fund Institute and the International Working Group of Sovereign Wealth Funds) to provide reassurance and transparency. The latter has published a set of investment guidelines called the Santiago Principles. By and large SWFs seem to be long-term, buy-and-hold investors. Besides, they played a crucial role in bailing out banks in the 2008 banking crisis: Citigroup, Merrill Lynch, Morgan Stanley and Barclays all turned to SWFs from China, Singapore, Kuwait and Abu Dhabi for equity injections. Between them these SWFs pumped in over $40 billion by way of fresh equity. In Citi's case it received over $14 billion, half of that from the Abu Dhabi Investment Authority alone.

Investment Management Styles

Having looked at the different types of fund and what they invest in (asset allocation) we'll look briefly at attitudes to investing itself.

Investment management is more an art than a science. It's about balancing risk against reward (return): *systemic risk* is market-wide; *specific risk* applies to an individual share or bond. If there were a magic alchemy that led to brilliant investment, everyone would try to find it and – of course – if everyone was practising it, it wouldn't work. For this reason markets are sometimes described as a **random walk**. No one has developed a fail-safe way to predict them.

Market professionals believe that what matters is not what the markets will do but what everyone else thinks they will do: if everyone thinks the market is going up, they will buy and it will go up – a self-fulfilling prophecy. This is called *market sentiment*. Markets react to expectations. They are forward-looking. They are said to *discount the future* – in other words to reflect in today's price expectations of what is likely to happen in the future. Again, market professionals say that what matters is not whether a share or a bond is a good investment but whether someone will be prepared to buy it from you for more than you paid.

None of this has dissuaded people from trying to perfect a gold-plated investment style. There are *chartists* (also known as *technical analysts*) who reduce market movements to spikes on graphs and try to predict the future from past spikes. They believe there are certain levels which if the market moves above or below indicate longer-term future moves. By contrast there are *momentum investors* who try to spot market moves that reflect underlying sentiment then jump aboard the market bandwagon – and jump off it again before it collapses (*trend following* is the same, using computers). There are *contrarians* who do the opposite of what they believe everyone else is doing.

Possibly the most successful style in recent years has been **value investing**. The idea is to find companies that are undervalued on their *fundamentals* (good product or service, good management, good brand, good markets with great potential; none of which is reflected in the current share price) then to buy shares in them and hold them for a long time. One exponent was Peter Lynch who ran Fidelity's flagship Magellan Fund. Another was Sir John Templeton who, with colleague Mark Mobius, specialised in emerging markets. Another is Warren Buffett (nicknamed the Wizard of Omaha), possibly the most famous investor in the world, whose investment fund, Berkshire Hathaway, made many investors into millionaires. He tended to buy few investments but take big stakes when he did and hold those investments for decades. The reason for his nickname was that Berkshire Hathaway was based in Omaha, Nebraska, deliberately so because he believed that keeping distant from the centres of the financial markets like New York made you a clearer-headed investor.

Possible Conflicts

Fund managers spend the bulk of their time looking for investment opportunities and visiting companies in which they have invested. They use *research* to decide what to buy in the markets. Research is provided by *analysts* who work for banks and brokers. They provide the research free in the hope that their clients, the investors, will trade on the basis of it and give them their buy and sell orders (from which banks and brokers earn a *commission* or, if selling or buying directly to or from the investor, a **spread**). This research can give rise to conflicts of interest. If a bank is advising an issuer on an equity issue, there is a temptation to encourage the banks' research analysts to write positive (buy) reports.

Another source of conflict can arise over **soft commissions** (outlawed in many markets) where a broker will offer a fund manager inducements to encourage the fund manager to funnel the fund's buy and sell orders through that broker. These inducements can range from corporate hospitality to Reuters screens (subscription-only trading data services) where the cost is borne by the broker. The point is that it is the fund's investors who pay for the brokerage (it is one of the costs that is charged to the fund) while the fund manager gets the benefit of the inducements.

Bank Services

Banks offer hedge funds an all-in-one service called **prime brokerage** which includes processing buy and sell orders, dealing in derivatives, providing over-the-counter tailored financial products, stock lending and short-term liquidity (loans).

Banks also offer pension funds and institutional investors a service called **custody** that looks after all their securities worldwide, including collecting coupons and dividends, turning them into the investor's home currency, dealing with any taxes, and safeguarding the securities themselves. Given the huge numbers of shares, bonds and other financial instruments that institutional investors hold, it's hardly surprising that they need help tracking their portfolios. It's made more complex by the different markets they invest in, with payment flows in different currencies and different local tax regimes to satisfy.

Custody is offered by a number of banks including trust banks. It can provide a steady source of fee income that offsets the fluctuations of trading gains and losses. But banks that do it well and profitably tend to have dedicated computer systems and networks of sub-custodian banks in markets throughout the world including emerging markets.

2   INTERMEDIARIES

Talk of banks takes us on to the second type of market participant, intermediaries (banks and brokers). Big banks lie at the heart of the markets.

A bank is, technically, an organisation that has a banking licence. But this definition tells you nothing. The biggest banks combine commercial banking (lending) with investment banking (helping issuers issue securities and trading those securities) and broking (buying and selling securities for institutional investors). They also manage money, like institutional investors (this is called asset management when a bank does it), and may offer pensions and insurance products (doing this is called banc assurance). The diagram below shows the anatomy of a bank that does everything. It's divided into three columns with commercial banking on the left, investment banking in the middle and banc assurance (insurance and pensions activity) on the right.

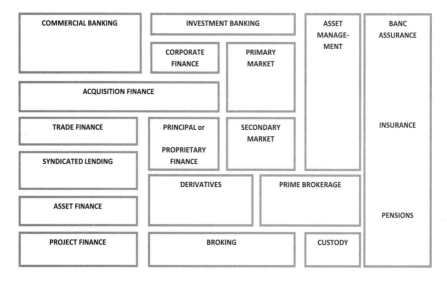

Under commercial banking we have acquisition finance (loans to help companies take over other companies), trade finance (helping companies finance exports), syndicated lending (loans to companies and governments that are too big for one bank to want to make), asset finance (finance leasing of big ticket items such as planes, ships, oil rigs and so on) and project finance (limited or non-recourse financing of infrastructure projects in emerging markets). Not shown here are commercial banks' retail operations which tend to be familiar to most people as bank customers.

Acquisition finance straddles investment banking too. That's because some takeovers are funded by short-term bond issues with high coupons (high-yield issues, in other words, but not junk) rather than loans and then refinanced later. So acquisition finance can fall under both commercial and investment banking.

Under investment banking we have corporate finance (helping companies raise equity funding through share issues and advising them on takeovers, also known as M&A – mergers and acquisitions), primary market activity (underwriting and distributing share and bond issues, also called origination or note issuance), secondary market activity (trading and making a market in the same), principal or proprietary finance (where the bank uses its own capital to buy businesses and realise their value through dismembering them and merging the constituent bits with other businesses while selling off non-core assets, for example), derivatives trading and creation (as OTC products) for corporate clients, and finally broking which is like secondary market trading activity but specifically for institutional investor clients. Derivatives shares its space with prime brokerage. Hedge funds are big users of derivatives and investment banks provide them with a variety of services through prime brokerage (see earlier).

Then on the right we have asset management (both retail and wholesale) and the provision of insurance and pensions (called banc assurance in mainland Europe where major German banks tend to do it) as well as custody (looking after institutional investors' securities and the interest, dividend, currency and tax aspects).

3 ISSUERS

The final market participants are issuers (companies in the case of shares and bonds; governments in the case of bonds). Issuers and intermediaries comprise the sell side.

Companies need capital (which simply means a pile of cash) for two things.

Profit

The first is to expand. It's a strange fact of business life that a company that isn't expanding, reaping economies of scale and making more profit, is going backwards: it risks being overtaken by competitors that are. In this sense money is like petrol in an engine. The more you have the faster and longer you can go. Companies will borrow money to expand rather than just use existing profit (called *retained earnings*) because borrowing enables them to expand more quickly. In particular, fast-growing companies – the ones that need a lot of petrol – don't usually have much surplus profit left over.

Cash Flow

The second is cash flow. Cash flow is the oil of their business engine. You can have a tank full of petrol and your foot flat on the floor but if you don't have enough oil in the engine it will seize up and break. Cash flow is, at its most simple, the ability of a business to pay its creditors (the people it owes money to) such as suppliers. If a company cannot meet its outgoings as they fall due (suppliers, staff, premises, running costs) it will cease to trade – no matter how profitable on paper that business is or could have been. Hence the expression 'cash is king'. It's lack of cash flow that causes most businesses to go bust, especially small, fast-growing ones.

Debt

Another strange aspect of business life is that companies are much bigger users of debt than individuals (except people who buy virtually everything on credit). This is because the cost of *servicing* debt (the interest payments) is generally *tax-deductible* as a business expense so reduces taxable profit, whereas paying dividends to shareholders is done out of *taxed profit* so is more expensive. This makes debt often cheaper to use than equity. The quid pro quo is that companies only pay dividends when they have enough profit out of which to do so, but they always have to pay interest on their debt.

Corporate Finance

Companies come to the City to do two things: to go from being a private company to a public one by floating on the stock exchange and raising more *equity finance* (by issuing fresh shares) while they are about it; and to take over other companies through M&A (mergers and acquisitions) for which they almost invariably need further funding too. Raising equity finance and M&A are bracketed together as **corporate finance** and investment banks and brokers do both (brokers for smaller companies, banks for bigger ones).

Takeovers (M&A)

Takeovers can generate a lot of press comment and are often resisted by the *target* company whose board of directors know they are likely to be terminated if the bid is successful. If so, they will reject the bid as being too low in which case the bid is said to become *hostile*.

The *bidder* will try to appeal to the target's shareholders, telling them to sell their shares in the target to the bidder in return for shares in the bidder. This way they become shareholders in a larger company that comprises the bidder and its newly-acquired subsidiary, the target, in which they were shareholders before. The bid will succeed if they believe the bidder will do a better job than the target's current management. The bidder will be hoping that the target's shareholders will accept its shares rather than a *cash alternative* since this will be cheaper for the bidder (printing shares is cheaper than borrowing money).

This is one reason why M&A is much easier to undertake as a public company (when your shares have an immediate value since they are quoted on the stock exchange) than if you are a private company (when they don't). Again, the reason for taking over another company is to expand more quickly.

Takeovers are policed in the City by the Takeover Panel and its rulebook is called the Takeover Code.

Venture Capital

The City can become involved with companies at an earlier stage of their development when they are still privately held, through something called **venture capital**, also known as *start-up* or *seed capital*. Businesses need a lot of cash as they get underway and build up a customer base and a product range. The *burn rate* is the speed with which they spend it. Venture capital houses (often owned by banks but, crucially, providing equity finance rather than debt) will *inject* equity capital in return for a shareholding.

Businesses are at their most vulnerable when they are expanding fast, their cash flow is poor, and they are using current income both to sustain existing operations and to build out the business. It's risky hence the term 'venture'. In fact on average two in three start-ups go bust in their first five years. For this reason a venture capital investor will want to take a large stake (shareholding) so that whatever it makes from a successful start-up more than offsets its losses from those that fail.

When the business is big and successful enough, there are four *exit routes* (ways) for a venture capital investor to *realise* its investment (sell the investment for cash):

- *Trade sale* (where the venture capital investor encourages the company to merge with another in a similar business).
- *Flotation* on the stock exchange.
- *Recycling* (where the venture capital investor sells its stake to another one which specialises in taking stakes in more established businesses).
- *Management buy-out* (where the founders buy back their stake, perhaps with funding from another venture capital provider).

In fact management buy-outs (MBOs) are used by successful bidders to dispose of parts of a target's business which are regarded as *non-core* – by selling them to their existing management.

A recent example of a start-up sector of particular relevance to financial markets is *fintech* which covers financial technology companies aiming to transform or disrupt traditional financial services.

Private Equity

No company is too big to be taken over. The threat may not be from another company but from a **private equity** house. One of the first private equity takeovers was that of RJR Nabisco by KKR (itself still one of the best known private equity firms) which was the subject of the book *Barbarians At The Gates*.

Private equity firms raise money privately (not through a stock exchange listing) from institutional investors (especially pension funds) in order to buy public companies' shares (equity). The idea is to buy all of the shares of a listed target in order to take it private (called *take privates*). It can then be broken up, the constituent businesses sold off and the rump re-listed. The aim is to do this in three years which is called a 'quick flip'. The reason for the hurry is that a lot of these deals are highly leveraged: a lot of the cash used to fund the takeover is borrowed so the quicker it's paid back, the lower the borrowing cost and the bigger the profit. Even if a deal isn't highly leveraged at the outset it's common for private equity investors to load the investee company up with debt and then to pay that money out to themselves in what is called *dividend recapitalisation*.

After the banking crisis many of these private equity firms found themselves having to manage businesses they couldn't easily re-sell, so they have become known as **alternative asset managers** (along with hedge funds). Venture capital itself is often now regarded as part of private equity.

The point about all of these takeovers (private equity and mainstream M&A) is that over a 10-year period as many as 60 per cent of the FTSE 100 will disappear. So the corporate world is very dynamic and forever changing.

Governments

Governments for their part are big borrowers because their only other source of money is taxation and at various times their tax receipts aren't sufficient for what they need to do, such as modernising public services and infrastructure (schools, hospitals, transport) or to meet the cost of supporting those out of work in a recession. So they borrow in order to pay back later.

So companies and governments are big users of the financial markets to get cash – to meet short-term cash flow gaps and longer-term investment needs. And they turn to banks to help them raise it.

We've looked at who the market participants are. Now we'll recap the instruments and transactions with which they get involved and look at what money actually is.

CHAPTER 12

MARKETS, MONEY AND MODELS

The three 'I's – issuers – intermediaries – institutional investors – capital diagram – equity story – lifecycle of a company – debt – loans – bonds – securitisation – derivatives – financial oceans – whales – shark – fish – actual market – fruit and vegetable market – customers: companies and governments – stallholders: banks – wholesalers: institutional investors – porters: brokers – money – double coincidence of wants – stockpiling of value – transportable – durable – divisible – standard – bullion – medium of exchange – liquid store of value – unit of account – stability – deferred payments – goldsmiths – portable – uniform – fungible – acceptable – confidence – international financial centres – international financial markets

We're nearly finished now. In this chapter I summarise the ways in which I see the financial markets – the models that work for me – and look at what money actually is.

In the last chapter we looked at the **three 'I's – the issuers, intermediaries and institutional investors** (four 'I's, if you prefer) which tells us *who* the market participants are. The **capital diagram** below summarises *what* instruments and transactions they get involved in.

Capital Diagram

At the top is capital – what you and I call money. On the left hand side is **the equity story** – the **lifecycle of a company** from venture capital to flotation, M&A, management buy-outs and private equity. Then on the right side we have **debt – the two types**. In the left hand column, commercial banking (**loan-based funding**) with investment banking (**bonds**) on the right with their different maturities. Then **securitisation** turns loans into bonds and at the bottom of the whole picture, straddling both, we have **derivatives** which can be derived from almost anything above and cover both equity and debt instruments. This picture helps me pigeon-hole new types of instrument as they come along.

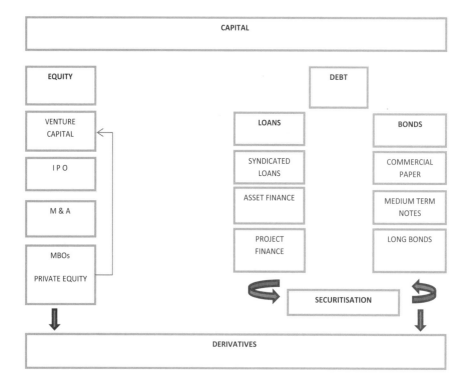

Financial Oceans

Another picture I have is of the three principal market participants (institutional investors, intermediaries, issuers) as inhabitants of the **financial oceans**. At the bottom are the **whales**. These are huge, shy and rarely seen. They are the institutional investors. It matters to them that the financial oceans are deep so they can move around without being spotted or disturbing the waters above them. Then, mid-way to the surface, are the intermediaries. They are banks and brokers. They are the market **porpoises** – fast and nimble. Then on the surface are issuers. These are the **fish** of the oceans and there are lots of them. Most are companies. But there are a smaller number of bigger ones. They are governments.

Fruit And Veg Market

Another picture I devised that people find helpful is that of the financial markets as an **actual market**. Picture a **fruit and vegetable market**. There are **customers**. They come to the market to buy fruit and veg. The stallholders sell the fruit and veg to them. The **stallholders** are kept stocked up by **wholesalers** who bring the fruit and veg from the local farms and ensure the stalls have produce. There are porters who move the fruit and veg between the wholesalers, the stallholders and the customers. The **customers are companies and governments**. They come to the market not to buy fruit and veg but to buy the use of money. The **stallholders are banks** who provide the money. The **wholesalers are institutional investors** who keep the banks' stalls stocked with money. The **porters are brokers**. But how can you use money to buy the use of money? Easy – with loans or bonds you pay interest for the use of the money. With shares you pay dividends. Note also that these days brokers can be parts of banks which is why the term intermediaries covers them both.

What Is Money?

Finally, this book is about the financial markets. But what is money and why do we use it? Imagine a primitive world without money. You have to barter for what you want. Let's say you grow potatoes but what you want is fish (for a more varied diet). Instead of getting on with growing your crop you have to spend time finding someone who not only has fish *but who wants potatoes in return*. This is what economists call a **double coincidence of wants**. And that's not the end of it. Having found that person you will only conclude a successful exchange if you can agree a price (how much fish for how many potatoes). One other problem: such activities don't permit the **stockpiling of value**. With both fish and potatoes what you can't eat or trade will rot. It will become valueless. You will never be able to build up a store of value to tide you over in retirement, so you won't be able to stop working.

As society developed, people used popular commodities such as sheep to pay for whatever they wanted to buy. But sheep are difficult to carry, don't last forever, can't be divided (you can't give a leg of mutton in change as you can 50p for a quid) and some are bigger and healthier than others. Salt was also used (the word 'salary' comes from the Latin 'salarium' for 'salt money') which had the merit of being **transportable**, **durable**, **divisible** and **standard**. But it can still get wet and not everyone wants it all the time. Then people switched to precious metals such as silver and gold (**bullion**) as currency. Currency provides a **medium of exchange** (in place of barter), a **liquid store of value** (it doesn't go off so you can stockpile it for the future), a **unit of account** (whereas sheep don't come in a standard size) and **stability** (it doesn't go out of fashion). It provides, therefore, a standard of **deferred payments** (you can buy now and promise to pay later). But gold isn't that portable and it isn't so divisible.

People entrusted their gold to **goldsmiths** (mentioned earlier) who gave them a receipt. When a depositor wanted to pay someone else, he wouldn't bother to go and get the gold: he'd simply hand over his receipt to the other for that person to claim the gold off the goldsmith. In practice it was much easier to leave the gold where it was in safe keeping and just exchange receipts. This is how money (paper notes) started. And the goldsmiths, knowing the gold would stay where it was, could lend it out by issuing further notes in respect of it, which is how banking started.

Nowadays we use coins and notes over gold because they are **portable, uniform** (which means that money is **fungible** – when you lend a friend a fiver, you don't expect that identical note back), **divisible**, **acceptable** (in the old days, some people didn't want sheep or salt) and **durable** (you can replace old coins and notes). In fact the old idea that paper money should be backed by reserves of gold has disappeared.

So, when you think about it, we use coins and notes because we have **confidence** in their value, not because they are a substitute for gold. Confidence (the sense that your money has value and you will get it back if you stick it in a bank) is critical to financial markets. Money is a funny thing when you think about it: a confidence trick. And confidence is the oxygen of the financial markets.

Bricks And Clicks

The final image I have of the markets, one I've mentioned before, is of the world's skies. At any one time there are thousands of planes in flight, going from one place to another. If you were to map them from space, they would probably appear as clouds over certain cities, which act as hubs for the world's airlines. As some ascend to join these clouds, others descend. This is the picture I want you to have of the world's financial markets.

The point of the picture is this: the cities over which these clouds hover are the world's **international financial centres**; the clouds themselves are the **international financial markets**. The international financial centres are the places where the people and the institutions for which they work – the market participants – are based. Overhead are the international financial markets, the clouds of financial transactions and instruments that they trade. The international financial centres are the *bricks*. The international financial markets are the *clicks*.

This picture for me represents the duality of the world's financial markets. On the one hand these markets are very real: people work in them and they and their institutions make a lot of real money – money you can spend in shops. Walk down Wall Street and the skyscrapers that house the world's biggest banks are real. These are the bricks.

On the other hand the financial markets are virtual. Some still have trading floors but mainly they exist in cyberspace, electronic entries on computer screens, deals agreed over the phone. The money here doesn't seem real – and in many respects it isn't. When a trader can take positions of hundreds of millions of dollars in the international financial markets every day, these amounts are so big you can't even imagine them. These are the clicks.

Airship Aloft

This book has been a giant airship. We've climbed aboard and it's taken us up into the clouds of the financial markets to get a good look at what these markets really are, at the instruments and transactions that like trillions of rain drops make up these clouds, and from there we've looked down at the international financial centres and their offshore counterparts, the offshore financial centres. Then, finally, as we've descended we've looked in through the windows of the tall skyscrapers and office buildings to look at the market participants – the institutional investors, intermediaries and issuers – and the individuals inside behind their desks, at their screens and on the phone.

Now we're just about to land again amongst the wider public, the people in the streets, people like you and me, whose money makes all of this possible. But before we do that we must address one final topic which is about protecting you and me, as investors and taxpayers. It's a topic that has dominated the headlines. It's regulation.

FINAL THOUGHTS

REGULATION – AND HOW TO READ THE *FINANCIAL TIMES*

Bank deposits – quantitative easing – Crash of 1929 – Glass-Steagall – Securities and Exchange Commission – no-action letters – too big to fail – moral hazard – Volcker rule – bail-in bonds – contingent convertible (co-co) bonds – living wills – stress tests – systemically important financial institutions – LIBOR and foreign exchange scandals – gold fix – insider dealing – insider trading – front running – market timing – late-trading – sticky assets – pump and dump – ramping – Ponzi – pyramid schemes – interest rate protection products – cap – interest rate swaps – share options – backdating – spring-loading – bullet-dodging – Bank of England – Prudential Regulation Authority – Financial Conduct Authority – Financial Times – main section – companies & markets section – supplements – Lex column

We've left regulation to last. Some books start with it. But that's like trying to explain what goes on in a village by starting with what the local policeman does. You need to know what the people in the village do to understand where, when and why they need regulating.

In fact, regulation is a hard subject to get your head around. There seem to be a plethora of initiatives, reviews, reports and inquiries under way and all sorts of agencies, commissions, government bodies, international taskforces and summits involved.

The principal role of the regulators and policy makers is to instil confidence in the financial markets. For instance **bank deposits** up to a substantial level are guaranteed by government (the Treasury in the UK) or state agencies (the Federal Deposit Insurance Corporation in the US). Otherwise individuals wouldn't leave their money with banks and there wouldn't be any money to lend out to businesses. After the global financial crisis, central banks around the world pumped liquidity (money) into the markets by printing money and using it to buy assets (such as bonds) from the markets, freeing banks up to lend more. This was called **quantitative easing**. Usually printing money is hugely inflationary. In this case it wasn't – a measure of the cash flow crunch the world was facing.

But the detailed regulation you find in all financial markets is really designed to do two things: protect big financial institutions from themselves; and protect us from them.

Protecting Them From Themselves

The global financial crisis of 2008 was caused by big banks going bust – just as they did in the **Crash of 1929**, which prompted the Depression of the 1930s (the purpose of quantitative easing was to stop a repeat of the latter).

The **Crash of 1929** was caused by commercial banks investing customers' deposits in the stock market. When it collapsed they couldn't pay depositors back and this led to runs on banks (when everyone rushed to get their money out) and bank failures. So in 1934 the US enacted legislation called **Glass-Steagall** (after the two politicians who led it) which said that banks could either be commercial banks or investment banks but not both. This is why the name Morgan ended up on three different institutions: JPMorgan, the commercial bank; Morgan Stanley, the investment bank (in those days called brokers) and Morgan Guaranty (a trust bank carrying out custodian activities).

The Glass-Steagall division between banking activities was policed by the US **Securities and Exchange Commission** (SEC), the US market watchdog. Over the next fifty years banks petitioned it: an investment bank seeking to do something that could have been seen as commercial banking would ask if it could. A commercial bank keen to do something approaching investment banking would do the same. The SEC would never say yes. The best it would say is: *If you do this we will take no action*. These **no-action letters**, as they were called, were public and had precedential value. In other words, any bank could act on what the SEC said.

By the 1990s Glass-Steagall was so riddled through with exemptions thanks to these no-action letters that it was actually repealed. The reasons for allowing banks this freedom were: one, their systems were now far better (so they claimed) at tracking their risk exposures; and, two, regulators were much more acute and joined up internationally to provide proper supervision.

Within 10 years the big banks had done it again. When the crisis hit in 2008 the biggest banks were both commercial banks (that is, they took in deposits and lent those deposits out) and investment banks (that is, they dealt in securities and increasingly took big positions on their own account as principal). When the investment banking arms went bust (because of these positions, specifically in mortgage-backed bonds) governments had to step in to save the deposit-taking arms. That's because they were said to be **too big to fail** – if allowed to fail they would have brought down the entire global financial system too.

So the banks were taken over by governments and effectively bailed out by us, the taxpayers. This led to widespread revulsion against bankers who were seen to have put other people's money (ours) at risk in order to earn themselves huge bonuses. And when it all went wrong they walked away and we picked up the tab. This is called **moral hazard**: encouraging reckless behaviour by providing safeguards against the risks.

The reforms since have pursued two aims. The first is to stop banks from certain types of proprietary trading (using money to take market positions for their own account, much as they did with sub-prime). This is, for example, what the **Volcker rule** does in the US. It's to stop investment banks behaving like 'casino banks' (to use an expression favoured by politicians, delighted that for once there are people even less popular than them). In the old days this wasn't as necessary because banks were partnerships owned by the individuals who worked in them. They were careful in what they did because it was their money and their liability if the bank failed. Nowadays the money is other people's – shareholders'.

The second is to make sure banks are strong enough in future not to require government bail-outs funded by taxpayers. Banks have always been required to maintain certain levels of regulatory capital (remember the cushion of capital mentioned in securitisation). Now, however, this requirement has been increased significantly by national and international regulators who are taking a much greater interest in the risk exposure of banks' loan books and their inventories of securities. Of course, banks hate this. Regulatory capital is dead money on which they are paying dividends to shareholders or interest to depositors or other banks. So this supervisory capital is a cost to them.

To help them meet these requirements, banks have been issuing **bail-in** and **co-co bonds** (short for **contingent convertible bonds**). Bail-in bonds require bondholders to give up their capital investment if the bank runs into trouble. Co-cos can suspend coupon payments and be converted into equity if the bank hits trouble. Instruments like these are intended to help avoid taxpayer bail-outs.

Banks have been subjected to **stress tests** by regulators all over the world. They've been required to draw up **living wills**, putting in place detailed plans for their orderly winding up ('resolution') if they run into trouble. There is also talk of imposing criminal liability on senior management for reckless behaviour, all designed to concentrate the mind.

In response to the 'too big to fail' concerns regulators have been identifying **systemically important financial institutions** (SIFIs) and subjecting them to additional requirements. Nor are they stopping at banks. Insurance companies and fund managers have been targeted.

AIG was the biggest insurer to go bust in the global financial crisis and that's because it had a financial products unit that was writing more credit default swaps than anyone else. These generate good fee income when markets are benign. But what AIG had overlooked was that when markets turn, defaults happen in bulk, not singly on their own. The global crisis triggered a flood of credit default claims. As they escalated AIG went under. So regulators argue that insurance companies can be SIFIs.

But why stop there? Asset managers handle hundreds of billions of dollars for investors. Doesn't this make them SIFIs too? Asset managers argue that they do not hold investors' money for themselves but instead that investors' funds are ringfenced under trust law.

Maybe. But one of the consequences of the increased capital requirements imposed on banks is that they are now less able than they were to commit capital to hold inventories of bonds and shares. This means that in times of market crisis there may be less liquidity available than market participants expect. So they may not be able to sell so easily and panic may ensue.

This risk has prompted regulators to look at markets more generally. For example, money market funds attract vast quantities of money because they are mutual funds which pay a better rate of interest than banks, while offering investors bank facilities such as easy withdrawals and deposit accounts. Would they effectively turn into SIFIs if mass redemptions threatened market meltdown?

Protecting Us From Them

The other purpose of regulation – in fact the purpose of most market regulation – is to protect innocent market users from hardened market professionals. This is what the **LIBOR and forex** (foreign exchange) **scandals** were about. Both involved the rigging of market rates, one the rate at which banks lend, the other the various rates at which currency trades are done ('fixing' is not fraudulent – it's the mechanism by which a rate is arrived at; 'rigging' the rate is what is fraudulent).

We saw earlier that forex dealers were sharing clients' orders and information in order to influence the rate at which the fix occurred. The LIBOR scandal was more technical. Here, roughly two dozen major banks would submit their cost of borrowing on a daily basis to the British Bankers Association (the BBA) in London. The BBA would discard the outliers (the top four and bottom four figures) and average the rest. This average then became the market rate for the next 24 hours. LIBOR was used as a reference far beyond the interbank market – hence the scandal when it was found to have been manipulated. Banks weren't being honest about their cost of borrowing. They were submitting quotes expressly to influence the average.

But it was not a clear-cut fraud. The rate rigging was uncovered at a time when banks' credit standings were fragile because of the global financial crisis. If a bank was completely honest about its cost of borrowing this could have alerted others banks to the fact that it wasn't considered creditworthy (your cost of borrowing is a direct reflection of your market standing). This in turn could have put them off lending to it, which in turn could have caused the very collapse that banks were trying to avoid. More than one bank argued that it was submitting inflated quotes so that it didn't end up in government hands, bailed out by the taxpayer. And when the BBA was stripped of responsibility for setting LIBOR, it for one was relieved. This was not a job it had particularly aspired to doing all along since it is a members' trade association, not a regulator.

The Gold Fix

In fact – and this is the most interesting aspect of the LIBOR and forex scandals – regulators began to ask what industry insiders were doing setting market rates at all. It's a bit like bakers getting together to decide what the daily price of a loaf of bread should be.

A good example is what happened to the gold market, which then became typical of what followed elsewhere. It's worth looking at in some detail to give you a flavour of how these things work.

Until surprisingly recently, the price of gold was fixed twice a day in London (the **gold fix**) by a group of six banks, each of which would send a representative round to merchant bank Rothschilds at 11 in the morning and 3 in the afternoon, armed with their customers' buy and sell orders. In front of each representative was a little flag to raise or lower until equilibrium between buys and sells had been reached. That then fixed the price of gold till the next fixing session. While the details had moved with the times (flags were replaced by the phone), the essence hadn't. In short there was no market unless those at the centre of it made it happen.

Following the FX scandal and regulators' response, the banks involved in the gold fix pulled out, for fear they would be accused of manipulating it. Without them of course there was no fix and no market. This had wider repercussions, affecting gold miners and bullion producers. They are naturally long of gold (they have reserves of it in the ground). So they need an active, liquid market in which they can short gold to hedge their long exposure. This in turn requires a daily rate that banks will honour. The gold fix has now been replaced by a semi-automatic averaging of market quotes that is administered by an exchange. Critics fear it may still be possible to influence the market.

Regulators are keen to see OTC markets, such as swaps, move on-exchange (using clearing houses known as 'central counterparties' to isolate default risk). The issue is whether on-exchange products have the depth of liquidity of OTC markets to absorb massive sell pressures at times of market disruption. Ironically, this risk is increased by the additional regulatory capital banks are required to have, which reduces their ability to hold inventories of commodities (such as gold) that provide market liquidity. Indeed banks have been selling off their commodity trading arms as a result.

The furore caused by the LIBOR and FX scandals is symptomatic of changing morality in the financial markets. This isn't anything new.

Insider Dealing / Trading

Before 1958, **insider dealing** or **insider trading** (the buying or selling of securities on the basis of information that isn't public) was perfectly legal in London (and in Tokyo until more recently). In fact, if asked, brokers would say that insider trading was how they made money. Why be in the market if you couldn't profit from it in this way? Indeed, how could there be a market unless people traded on inside information? So with LIBOR and with forex, just as with Lloyd's of London. All of these were different members-only clubs. But of course their actions affect a far wider constituency.

Insider dealing is a crime carried out either directly or by tipping off others who act on the information. It occurs most often prior to the announcement of an M&A deal: since the bidder is going to want the target's shares, they will go up in price as soon the bid is announced. A price spike just prior to the announcement is the tell-tale sign. Stock exchanges are as diligent in pursuing insiders as the authorities are, for reputational reasons – investors won't want to use a market where share prices are adversely affected by insider trading. However, convictions are hard to achieve since the passing on of tips doesn't leave much of an evidential trail.

Other Market Abuses

Of course, there are plenty of other professional scams but these attract less interest because they are more technical and less brazen. **Front running** occurs where a broker trades for its own account before filling a client's order, knowing that the client's order will move the market in its favour. Front running can occur in many markets (a variation of it happened in the FX scandal).

Market timing and **late-trading** are specific to fund management and occur where a mutual fund (unit trust) allows favoured investors (usually market traders) to buy units at prices below their actual value, based on valuations of the underlying assets that are no longer current. These scams hit the headlines in New York in 2003 involving over 20 funds managing over a fifth of US mutual fund assets. Shockingly, webs of collusion were unearthed where investors (often hedge funds) left **sticky assets** in one fund in return for beneficial trading in another, related fund. More everyday are **pump and dump** strategies (also known as stock **ramping**) where positive, but false, rumours are spread about a stock that can then be sold at a profit in the upwards price momentum that the rumours cause.

Ponzi And Pyramid Schemes

The bulk of financial services regulation is aimed at protecting investors – hence the extensive regulations in all countries governing the promotion (selling) of securities to the public, and the requirements that stock exchanges impose on companies listed on them to provide regular, comprehensive and correct financial information. The retail market is always open to abuse. Financial markets attract fraudsters because – to misquote Jesse James – that's where the money is.

So, for example, Allen Stanford was gaoled in 2012 for 110 years over a $7 billion fraud that wrecked the island of Antigua and the livelihood of its people since he controlled most of Antigua's economy, including its largest bank.

Bernard Madoff was gaoled in 2009 for 150 years for defrauding his clients of $50 billion – even by today's standards a staggering amount of money. Madoff's fraud, like most, was a **Ponzi** scheme (taking in money from new investors and using it to pay out above-market returns to old investors) named after Charles Ponzi who did this in the 1920s. Perhaps most shocking of all, Madoff was a former chairman of NASDAQ.

Madoff was offering consistent returns of 10%. Typical scams involve the promise of, on the one hand, investment in safe instruments such as government securities with, on the other, a level of return which such safe investments simply can't generate. It takes a sucker to be suckered. The only extraordinary thing is how often governments have been forced to bail out victims of their own greed.

A variation on the Ponzi is the **pyramid scheme** where current investors are incentivised to find new ones whose money effectively pays them out (like a chain letter). These were popular in the 1990s in former east European countries where free markets were introduced without sufficient protection for the public. Romanian savers lost about $1 billion between 1991 and 1994 in the Caritas scheme. Two thirds of the Albanian population invested in pyramid savings plans that collapsed in 1997, prompting the overthrow of the government and intervention by the IMF (International Monetary Fund).

Rate Protection Insurance

To my mind the most pernicious scandal that banks have indulged in recently took place in the retail market. This concerned the sale of **interest rate protection products** to small businesses. Borrowers were sold insurance that (they were told) protected them against interest rate rises. They thought they were buying a **cap** – a guarantee that the interest rate on their loan wouldn't go above a certain point. In fact they were sold **interest rate swaps**, so that if interest rates went up they would be protected. But, crucially, if interest rates fell they would have to pay the difference. They were sold these things in the post-banking-crisis environment of falling interest rates as governments tried to stimulate these economies. So, far from their interest liabilities being capped, they ended up paying out more as interest rates fell. Some of these borrowers had to pay out so much under these swaps that they lost their entire businesses.

Issuer Share Option Scams

The corporate world isn't above sharp practice of its own, especially in awarding **share options** to senior management to incentivise them (the share options are only in the money when the company's share price hits a new, supposedly aspirational, level). Examples include **backdating** (setting the exercise price by reference to a previous low share price so it is automatically in the money), **spring-loading** (granting share options immediately before announcing good news that is bound to lift the share price and put the options in the money) and **bullet-dodging** (delaying a grant of options until after bad news is announced, so the exercise price can be made correspondingly low).

A Rock And A Hard Place

You could say that the most recent crises are a failing of regulation. But the regulators' job is tough. The first thing is that no matter how stringent the rules if people want to break them they will. Regulators are always at one remove – they are always outside the institutions they are seeking to supervise. They recruit from the same talent pool as the banks but can't pay anything like the same rewards. And their jobs are thankless. When things are going well, no one notices. When things go wrong you're in the front line.

In any case regulators are often constrained by structural issues. At the time of the 2008 crisis the UK wasn't helped by the way – since changed – that responsibility for economic and financial stability was shared between government (the Treasury for economic policy and the trade department for insurance company supervision), the **Bank of England** (monetary policy, financial stability) and the Financial Services Authority (market regulation and bank supervision).

The Bank of England as the central bank had traditionally been responsible for bank supervision but as it shouldered more of the burden for monetary policy (money supply and interest rates) so its prudential supervisory role was split three ways between it, government and the then FSA (now replaced by the **Prudential Regulation Authority** covering market stability and the **Financial Conduct Authority** for enforcement and consumer protection). When Northern Rock went bust there was paralysis at the centre which didn't help calm markets.

This idea of a patchwork of regulators with overlapping responsibilities is not unusual. It's the norm. Take the States. There is the Fed (the Federal Reserve, the US central bank) and then a further 12 regional Feds across the US. There is the SEC (Securities and Exchange Commission) but its remit does not extend to derivatives. They are supervised by the CFTC (Commodity Futures Trading Commission) because of their origin as options, forwards and futures in agriculture, buying and selling crops forward to guard against spikes in production or demand.

Then there are state insurance comptrollers and the Federal Deposit Insurance Corporation. But a lot of power is vested in the head of the New York Department of Financial Services, New York's top banking regulator. With so many competing regulatory bodies in the mix it's easier rather than harder for things to slip between the cracks.

Now imagine this internationally because, above all, the financial markets are international. Money flows like water between financial centres, seeking better returns however momentary they may be. But regulation is predominantly country-based. It is a bank's home country's job to monitor it worldwide. Obviously national regulators talk to each other all the time and meet in international committees. But there is no overarching supranational superstructure off which these things hang, just as the UN is not empowered to stop all conflicts, nor the IMF to bail anyone and everyone out. The world just doesn't work like that – yet.

HOW TO READ THE *FINANCIAL TIMES*

The FT comes in two parts, the **main section** and the **companies & markets section**. There may also be **supplements** – for instance, various surveys that are country or sector specific (such as Brazil or the Motor Trade). The first thing to do is to bin the supplements (many of them are advertising driven) unless you happen to be interested in the subject (the FT's supplements, it has to be said, are better than most).

Next, read the **Lex column**, on the back page of the first section. It is written by the FT's best young writers and is read by captains of industry, bankers, politicians and other opinion formers. After a while you detect a pattern. If they are commenting on X plc, a company that has just unveiled sparkling results, the piece will be along the lines of 'how much longer can they keep this up – must be heading for a fall.' If it's on Y plc, a bombed-out stock, the word will be 'can only get better from here.'

Next, read the first few pages of the second section (companies & markets) – you'll know when to stop because half-way through the words run out and it turns into figures, reporting stock, commodity and currency markets globally.

So put the second section to one side and read the first section – glance at the front page, then read it from back to front. Unless you're fascinated by geopolitics and the latest round of trade talks, it gets progressively more boring the closer you get to the front.

Next, turn back to the remaining pages of the second section (the ones covered in numbers) and scan this with a serious look on your face. This stage is optional and depends on whether you want your fellow commuters to think you really have an investment portfolio.

The index opposite also serves as a glossary. Turn to the page where a term is first mentioned and that should be where its meaning is given.

INDEX / GLOSSARY

O

P